A CALL TO EXCELLENCE

A Call to EXCELLENCE

Gary Inrig

While this book is designed for the reader's personal use and profit, it is also intended for group study. A leader's guide with visual aids (Victor Multiuse Transparency Masters) is available from your local bookstore or from the publisher.

VICTOR BOOKS a division of SP Publications, Inc.
WHEATON, ILLINOIS 60187

Offices also in
Whitby, Ontario, Canada
Amersham-on-the-Hill, Bucks, England

Second printing, 1986

Unless otherwise indicated, Scripture quotations are from the *New American Standard Bible*, © the Lockman Foundation 1960, 1962, 1963, 1968, 1971, 1972, 1973, 1975, 1977. Other quotations are from the *Holy Bible, New International Version* (NIV), © 1973, 1978, 1984, International Bible Society and used by permission of Zondervan Bible Publishers; and the *King James Version* (KJV). Used by permission.

Recommended Dewey Decimal Classification: 248.4
Suggested Subject Heading: CHRISTIAN LIFE: CHARACTER

Library of Congress Catalog Card Number: 84-52029
ISBN: 0-89693-523-X

CONTENTS

FOREWORD

"Talent is cheap; dedication is costly!" Evangelicalism needs to hear this message, for we are in danger of producing a manageable mediocrity, one whose slogan is, "Anything is good enough for God."

At last, a call to disdain what is cheap, trashy, and impermanent comes from Gary Inrig. Furnishing a fresh and realistic alternative, he steers a course between the extremes of feverish, compulsive activity and frustrating apathy, between carnal competition and casual indifference.

Christian excellence is not a vicious one-upmanship with others, but a personal commitment to becoming the best one can be. Achievement of high personal integrity—skill on the job, in parenthood, church life, and every level of functioning—is possible by God's enabling grace. It does not minimize individual differences, but rather magnifies being distinctively unique.

The quality of one's Christian life is in direct proportion to one's commitment to excellence. Goodness is not an option but an essential. "Whatever you do, work at it with all your heart, as working for the Lord, not for men" (Col. 3:23, NIV).

It is refreshing to recommend a tightly reasoned book written by one who fleshes out what he writes. To serve the author as professor and advisor on his doctoral dissertation has allowed me to know him as a student. Now as a colleague in ministry, I rejoice in Dr. Inrig's personal commitment to excellence and superb contribution to the body of Christ.

Here is a book intellectually stretching, biblically insightful, and personally motivating. *My suggestion:* Read it carefully and reflectively, as if Gary Inrig were speaking directly to you. He is. *My hope:* That it will revolutionize your life and ministry.

HOWARD G. HENDRICKS, PROFESSOR
DALLAS THEOLOGICAL SEMINARY

To Janice, Stephen, and Heather
with the prayer
that their lives may reflect
the excellence of
their Lord.

PREFACE

"Praise the Lord in song, for He has done excellent things; let this be known throughout the earth."

(Isa. 12:5)

The excellence of God is a truth which the writers of Scripture celebrate and in which believers rest and rejoice. The God of Scripture is excellent in all His character and perfect in all His ways, and the Lord Jesus Christ is the incarnation of the divine excellence.

Christians bear a high and holy responsibility—to serve in the world as ambassadors of Christ. Because we represent Him, what we are reflects on Him. Unbelievers form their opinions of our God from what they see in us. We may wish that this were not the case, but it is, and therefore we Christians must live lives worthy of our Lord. This necessarily involves a commitment to excellence, since our God is excellent.

What is excellence and what difference will it make in our lives? Those are the questions I try to address in this book. One idea is central. Excellence is not a great achievement or a marvelous performance. True excellence is a way of life. It touches all that we are and all that we do. Too often excellence is thought of in the narrowest of terms. An athlete pursues a championship trophy; a businessman seeks a quality product; an author strives to develop his skills as he works on his masterpiece. But this striving may not flow over into other areas of life. The result is impressive accomplishments but an

9

inconsistent life. True excellence, which reflects the character of our God, touches all of life until it becomes a way of life.

To write a book on excellence seems presumptuous. Certainly, I make no pretense of being anything other than a distant pursuer. The fact is that none of us, however gifted or accomplished, will attain excellence in this life. It is not so much a destination as a direction, from which none of us are exempt. In any sphere of life and in every sphere of life God calls us to display His excellence and to lay hold of His purpose. My prayer is that this book will help you understand what God's call to excellence means in your life's circumstances, and that it will inspire within you a deep desire to pursue such excellence.

I am deeply thankful to the Lord for many who have helped in various ways to make this book possible. In recent months, my mother has gone to be with her Lord. To her and my father I owe a debt which can never be repaid, and from the lives of both I have learned lessons about excellence. This material was first presented to my family in Christ at Bethany Chapel and I am very thankful for their encouragement, suggestions, and patience. Joanne Landry is due special thanks for her tireless and invaluable work in typing and editing this manuscript and the dissertation on which it is based.

Howard Hendricks is the man whom the Lord used to plant a love for the idea and the pursuit of excellence. Thousands of graduates from Dallas Theological Seminary bear eloquent witness to the way he has modeled excellence in his life and teaching, and I gladly take my place among them. I value greatly his help, encouragement, and friendship.

This material was originally presented as a dissertation to the faculty of Dallas Theological Seminary, as part of the requirements of the Doctor of Ministry program. I thank them for their permission to publish it in revised form, and thank God for their continuing model of excellence.

Above all, thanks are due to my wife, Elizabeth, who is truly the excellent wife of Proverbs 31 to me. Her encouragement and thoughtful observations have been especially valuable. "The heart of her husband trusts in her, and he will have no lack of gain" (Prov. 31:11). Special thanks also to my three delightful children, who have shown much patience and support during the process of turning this book into reality.

CHAPTER ONE

CALLED TO EXCELLENCE

Excellence is a powerful word. It conjures up images of great performances and soaring achievements. It brings to mind names and faces drawn from almost every walk of life—athletes, musicians, writers, politicians, entertainers, thinkers, teachers—which evoke admiration as well as inspiration. We not only value excellence in others, we desire it for ourselves.

Excellence is also a fashionable word. Politicians use it of themselves, declaring their ability to lead their nations to new levels of glory. Advertisers claim it for products ranging from linoleum to limousines, aware that we are a generation of consumers grown weary of planned obsolescence and plastic disposables. Corporations, colleges, and football coaches proclaim their commitment to excellence, while television extravaganzas celebrate what they claim to be examples of excellence. Excellence is "in." Everyone loves excellence and shuns mediocrity.

And so they should. People or companies or nations who do not set high standards and set out to achieve them will soon be left behind in a world of accelerating social and technological change. Human history is full of examples of dynamic movements which began to coast on past momentum and, as a result, declined, first into impressive monuments and finally into distant memories. There are also multitudes of minor tragedies, men and women with brilliant prospects whose lives display unrealized potential and unfulfilled promise. Ex-

11

cellence is not achieved by accident. What we aim at determines what we will become, and while we may not always make our goals, our goals will always make us. Therefore, to aim at excellence is to point one's life toward the realization of one's potential, the fulfillment of one's capabilities.

Excellence is therefore both socially valuable and personally desirable. But a Christian has a reason to pursue excellence which far transcends such man-centered viewpoints. For when a believer is called to the Lord Jesus Christ, he is also called to excellence, to be the best that he can be for his Saviour. The God of excellence calls His people to live lives of excellence, which reflect His character to this world. In every area of life, the Christian's goal must be to become what the Lord Jesus desires. God's purpose is to take our God-given potential and bring it into reality as we live for His glory. That being the case, there is no room for mediocrity or apathy.

The call to excellence has many facets. Excellence, to be pursued, must be understood, and a study of the biblical concept of excellence reveals that God's definition of excellence differs significantly from the world's. Almost inevitably, we think of excellence in terms of performance, but the Bible puts the emphasis elsewhere. But before the unique nature of biblical excellence is explored, the divine calling to Christian excellence needs to be confronted. In his letter to the believers in Colossae, the Apostle Paul provides a comprehensive introduction to the essential themes of our study:

> For this reason also, since the day we heard of it, we have not ceased to pray for you and to ask that you may be filled with the knowledge of His will in all spiritual wisdom and understanding, so that you may walk in a manner worthy of the Lord, to please Him in all respects, bearing fruit in every good work and increasing in the knowledge of God; strengthened with all power, according to His glorious might, for the attaining of all steadfastness and patience; joyously giving thanks to the Father, who has qualified us to share in the inheritance of the saints in light (Col. 1:9-12).

Colossae, in the old Roman province of Asia (now part of modern Turkey), was probably the least important town to which a New Testament epistle is addressed. Paul himself had never visited the city. But during the apostle's two-year ministry in Ephesus, Christians spread through the entire region preaching the Gospel, "so that all who lived in Asia heard the Word of the Lord, both Jews and Greeks" (Acts 19:10). It was a man named Epaphras who was instrumental in evangelizing Colossae (Col. 1:7) and the neighboring communities of Laodicea and Hierapolis. For a time the little church in Colossae experienced growth and blessing, but then Epaphras brought word to Paul that a serious crisis had developed—ideas alien to the Gospel were being embraced by many of the young believers. Alarmed, Paul wrote a letter which is both an explanation and a warning. His theme is stated succinctly in Colossians 1:18: "so that He Himself [the Lord Jesus] might come to have first place in everything." God's purpose for creation and the church is the unrivaled preeminence of Jesus Christ, a purpose overarching all human history and which must be translated personally into the present lives of believers. It is in view of that great theme that Paul prays as he does, and it is important to notice the structure of his prayer. He first states his *petition* (Col. 1:9): "that you may be filled." He then states the *purpose* of his petition (v. 10a): "so that you may walk in a manner worthy of the Lord, to please Him." He then concludes with the *products* which will result as this prayer is answered, using four parallel participles in the Greek text in verses 10-12: "bearing fruit; increasing; strengthened; joyously giving thanks." In turn, these elements of his prayer contain the source, the essence, and the evidence of Christian excellence.

THE SOURCE OF EXCELLENCE: THE PETITION

There are times when we find it necessary to pray for Christians we have never met. What do we ask for in such cases? Paul's prayer provides a model. He had heard a report from Epaphras that these Colossian Christians were characterized by faith in the Lord Jesus, love for fellow believers, and hope based on the promises of the Gospel. Such things are the living fruit of God's life in the believer. "For this reason also, since the day we heard, we have not ceased to pray for you and ask that you may be filled" (Col. 1:9). Paul's consistent, specific prayer life is itself a model of excellence, but it is

A CALL TO EXCELLENCE

important to see that Paul's prayer is not addressed to a special group of supersaints. Rather, it is a prayer for believers unknown to Paul, containing the essence of what he longed for in the lives of all God's people. Epaphras, who knew these Christians, had a very similar perspective. Paul assures the Colossians that he is "always laboring earnestly for [them] in his prayers, that [they] may stand perfect and fully assured in all the will of God" (Col. 4:12).

It is important not to miss the significance of this. At the basis of God's desire for the believer is "that [he] may be filled with the knowledge of His will in all spiritual wisdom and understanding." This is a prayer to be prayed, not only for believers we do not know, but for ourselves as well. It is here that we confront the source of spiritual excellence. But what exactly do we ask for when we ask to be "filled with the knowledge of His will"?

The will of God is, in its simplest form, the declaration of God's intention for His creatures. In this context, Paul has in view the moral will of God, revealed in the written Word of God. Of course, Paul writes these words before the New Testament, as we now possess it, was completed and collected. But he was aware, not only of the superintending work of the Holy Spirit as he wrote his letters (e.g., 1 Cor. 14:37), but also of the complete sufficiency of the Scriptures, which are written so "that the man of God may be adequate, equipped for every good work" (2 Tim. 3:17). The significance of that insight is overwhelming. God's Word contains all that the believer needs to know about the will of God, so as to live the way God desires. In the words of the psalmist:

Oh, how I love Your law!
    I meditate on it all day long.
Your commands make me wiser than my enemies,
    for they are ever with me.
I have more insight than all my teachers,
    for I meditate on Your statutes.
I have more understanding than the elders,
    for I obey Your precepts (Ps. 119:97-100, NIV).

But Paul is asking for more than an awareness of the will of God. His prayer is that we may be "filled with the knowledge of His will." The knowledge he prays for is not the intellectual accumulation of information, but an intimate personal knowledge. After almost twenty years of marriage, I possess much more than intellectual information about my wife's desires, obtained by scientific observation and reading books on the psychology of women. That kind of knowledge may have its place, but I know and love my wife. And that's the way a believer ought to be related to his Lord. We know His will because we know Him! And possessing such intimate personal knowledge of our Father's will, we should be "filled" with it. When we speak of someone being filled with anger or joy, we mean that he or she is controlled by that emotion. Likewise, a believer who is filled with the Holy Spirit is controlled and directed by the indwelling Helper. Thus Paul prays that believers will be filled and controlled by an intimate knowledge of God's will, which we find in His Word.

The application to the subject of excellence is very direct. As we shall see, excellence requires a standard at which to aim. Several years ago, we traveled as a family for a period of ministry in Australia. As a friend drove us (on the "wrong" side of the road!) from the airport into Melbourne, everything seemed rather strange and intimidating. What should we expect and could we adjust? Suddenly there was a shout of delight from the backseat. There, on the other side of the world, were the familiar Golden Arches. Ronald McDonald was alive and well and living in Australia! The vote was unanimous from the backseat—that's where they wanted their first meal. Having been assured by a Big Mac that some things were the same everywhere, we were ready for the challenge of the land of kangaroos and koalas. But it's part of McDonald's special form of excellence that its restaurants, everywhere in the world, measure up to its uniquely American standards.

Excellence in living also requires a standard. But from where are values and standards derived? Expertise isn't excellence—we are drowning in experts. For the Christian, the answer is found in the revealed will of God, His written Word. While the Scriptures do not answer specific questions about excellence, they do provide the essential principles for all forms of it.

Paul also notes that a life filled with the knowledge of God's will will be characterized by "all spiritual wisdom and understanding." Understanding refers to the ability to decide which principles apply in a given situation, while wisdom lays hold of the basic principles on which life should be based. Both words direct our attention to a great Old Testament idea—that of true wisdom. The Hebrew word for wisdom, *hokmah*, conveys the idea of skill. For example, a craftsman such as Bezalel, the major builder of the tabernacle, who had abilities as a metal worker, engraver, designer, embroiderer, and weaver, is said to have been filled with skill (literally, wisdom) to perform these tasks (Ex. 35:34-35). Furthermore, the word is used to describe the practical ability to lead and direct people, such as Solomon possessed (1 Kings 3:28; 4:29-30). As one scholar observes, "The primary reference of *hokmah* is to unusual skill or ability, to expertness of a particular kind, attained by training and experience added to special gifts."[1] To be "wise" is to have mastered your subject.

In its most important use, wisdom refers to moral skill, the practical ability to live as God intended. Wisdom is woven into the very fabric of the universe since "the Lord by wisdom founded the earth" (Prov. 3:19). Hence a wise person is one who conforms his life to God's order as found in His creation and in His Word. Basic to skill in living is a proper relationship to the Lord since reverence for Him is the beginning, the controlling principle, of wisdom (Prov. 9:10). Wisdom in the Old Testament is virtually a synonym for excellence. To live with skill is to live with excellence.

Wisdom touches every area of life and conduct, but primarily it is displayed in a person's character. This is the fundamental biblical perspective on excellence, since character is the source of actions. The excellence of a life is seen primarily in what a man is, and is, in turn, expressed in every role, relationship, or responsibility a person sustains. A wise person has mastered life because his life is lived in fellowship with the Master. A life of excellence is not so much the ability to do things well as it is the ability to live life well, in fellowship with God Himself.

THE ESSENCE OF EXCELLENCE: GOD'S PURPOSE
Paul does not end his prayer with the petition that believers "may be filled with the knowledge of His will in all spiritual wisdom and understanding." His prayer has a specific pur-

pose: "so that you may walk in a manner worthy of the Lord, to please Him in all respects." Paul's words contain both the standard of excellence (walking worthy) and the motivation for it (pleasing the Lord), and it is important that these are the result of a life filled with the knowledge of God's will.

THE STANDARD OF EXCELLENCE. God's desire is that every Christian should walk in a manner worthy of the Lord Jesus. The term *worthy* is a picture word, conveying the idea of balancing the other beam of the scales. In other words, what is worthy is what measures up to a standard. For the believer, the standard of measurement is never people-centered, but always Christ-centered. We are not to measure our lives by what others have done, but by what the Lord has done. We are to walk worthy of our heavenly calling (Eph. 4:1); to live worthy of the Gospel of Christ (Phil. 1:27); to walk worthy of God (1 Thes. 2:12). All of this is a response of gratitude to the grace and goodness of God.

The New Testament is rich in its vocabulary of excellence, a vocabulary which consistently points to the Lord Jesus as the standard of excellence. It is striking though that the usual Greek term for excellence, *arete*, occurs only five times. Almost certainly, the reason is that the Greek idea of excellence was man-centered in its orientation. Excellence meant the perfecting of oneself, based on human ability and achievement. This same perspective dominates virtually all modern discussions. Humanistic excellence is self-originated and man-centered, while biblical excellence points to God Himself as the standard and source of excellence. Therefore, the more common biblical way to describe excellence relates to the Greek term *telos*. The word describes the end or purpose of something, and the Scriptures use the term to remind us that God has made us with a *telos:* a purpose and a goal. To move toward this *telos* is to move toward wholeness, maturity, and excellence. Ultimate excellence awaits the Rapture, but relative excellence, i.e., spiritual maturity, is a constant possibility.

There is an appropriate level of maturity for every stage of development. As my children grow, I delight in their maturity. But the maturity of a ten-year-old is not that of a sixteen-year-old, nor of a forty-year-old. In a sense, we never reach full maturity—I find many areas of my life where true maturity remains a distant desire. So too, ultimate excellence awaits the time when we are with the Lord. But we can aspire to an appropriate level of excellence here and now, a pursuit inspired not merely by a man-centered desire for the fulfillment of our potential or the realization of our aspirations. The Christian's ultimate motivation is the fulfillment of the Father's purpose and the promotion of His glory, so as to live worthy of Him.

THE MOTIVE FOR EXCELLENCE. "To please Him in all respects"—that is the compelling desire. Every area of our lives becoming worthy of the Lord and bringing pleasure to Him— that is the heartbeat of excellence. For a businessman or homemaker or student or athlete, the expression of excellence will differ. But in our varied spheres of responsibility, we seek to please the Lord and promote His glory. "Therefore we have as our ambition to be pleasing to Him," Paul wrote to the Corinthian church (2 Cor. 5:9), and that perspective drove him to repudiate mediocrity as an adequate expression of Christian living. It is not enough to meet the requirements. A Christian abounds and excels because he wants to please the Lord. Nowhere does Paul state this more powerfully than to the Thessalonians. They were a group of Christians with whom he was delighted, the only congregation he calls a model church (cf. 1 Thes. 1:6-8). Nevertheless, he challenges them with the words of 1 Thessalonians 4:1: "Finally then, brethren, we request and exhort you in the Lord Jesus, that, as you have received from us instruction as to how you ought to walk and please God (just as you actually do walk), that you may excel still more." Paul was not writing to people who were falling short in their Christian lives. They were already living in a way that pleased God. But the status quo was not enough. His call is to abound, to excel, to press on, to aspire far more. Even excellence isn't enough: "excel still more." So important is Paul's charge that he repeated it in verse 10: "We urge you, brethren, to excel still more." Abundance is the standard of Christian living and pleasing God is the motivation. Such a perspective has no place for self-congratulation or complacency.

Two things ought to be observed about pleasing God. First, *the Lord knows us*, with our individual abilities and circumstances. He asks only for our best, without comparison to others. Second, *the Lord loves us*. He is not hard to please. A mother receives the artwork of her kindergarten child on Mother's Day, a picture in which only a parent could see beauty, and tapes it with pride to the refrigerator door. She sees excellence and beauty where others see only confusion and scribbles. Because she knows and loves her daughter, she is not hard to please. And God responds to our pursuit of excellence, from a desire to please Him, in the same way.

The basis of true excellence is love for God. We are told that a young painter once brought a painting of Christ to the nineteenth-century French artist Gustav Doré, seeking his approval. Doré was slow to comment. The artist was obviously skilled, but Doré's expert eye noted a fatal lack. Finally the master painter gave his verdict: "You don't love Him, or you would paint Him better." Skill alone does not produce excellence. And, as God measures excellence, there can be none where there is not a desire to walk worthy of the Lord, so as to please Him in all respects.

THE EVIDENCE OF EXCELLENCE

Paul concludes his brief prayer with a series of four participles which show the components of an excellent life. When a believer is filled with the knowledge of God's will, his life will possess attributes which provide a brief profile of excellence.

The first mark of an excellent life is *productivity:* "bearing fruit in every good work." Fruit is the natural product of the life of a tree, and in the same way, spiritual fruit is the inevitable product of God's life in the believer. The Lord Jesus placed a high priority on spiritual fruit-bearing, reminding us, "By this is My Father glorified, that you bear much fruit, and so prove to be My disciples" (John 15:8). Specifically, the fruit here is said to be good works. The Christian is created for good works (Eph. 2:10); the Lord redeemed us to be zealous for good works (Titus 2:14). However, it should be observed that good works are not the root of excellence, but the fruit of it. A believer properly related to his God will produce God's works.

The second mark is *progress:* "increasing in the knowledge of God." A controlling knowledge of God's will leads to the personal knowledge of the God whose will it is. This is the greatest privilege of life and none was more convinced than Paul of "the surpassing value of knowing Christ Jesus my

Lord" (Phil. 3:8). If knowing God is truly earth's greatest value, then no life can be excellent which is not growing into a deeper fellowship with the living God. As the Lord Himself says, through Jeremiah, "Let not a wise man boast of his wisdom, and let not the mighty man boast of his might, let not the rich man boast of his riches; but let him who boasts boast of this, that he understands and knows Me, that I am the Lord who exercises loving-kindness, justice, and righteousness on earth; for I delight in these things" (Jer. 9:23-24).

The third mark is *power:* "strengthened with all power, according to His glorious might, for the attaining of all steadfastness and patience." The power of which Paul speaks is not raw might—the ability to do great acts, so much as inner enablement—the ability to meet life's demands. And the measure of such power is God's omnipotence. He doesn't merely start us off and then leave us to do the rest, like someone pushing a child on a swing. His power is continuous and undiminished, through the presence of His indwelling Spirit. It is significant to observe the purpose of God's power. It is not for extricating us from every difficulty or for removing every obstacle, but rather "for the attaining of all steadfastness and patience." God's power is supremely revealed as a Christian patiently endures in the difficult experiences of life.

The fourth mark Paul describes is *praise:* "joyously giving thanks to the Father, who has qualified us to share in the inheritance of the saints in light." An attitude of thankful praise to God overflows into a positive, optimistic outlook on life. A believer whose heart is dominated by the grace of God will face all of life with confidence in the goodness of God.

It would be hard to find a better description of a person of excellence than one who is productive, progressive, powerful, and positive in spirit. But it must be recognized that these evidences of excellence are the product of a commitment to walk "worthy of the Lord, to please Him in all respects." In turn, that type of life requires the Christian to be filled with the knowledge of God's will. Obedience to God lies at the heart of all excellence, and an itching desire to please God is indispensable to the pursuit of excellence.

The great violinist Isaac Stern was once asked by a reporter, "What truly distinguishes a great musician?" Stern's reply was perceptive: "A great musician is one who is always seeking to improve, never content with his performances, always moving on to discover more about the instrument and the music he loves." On a far deeper level, the believer comes with the same attitude to his Lord. We are called to excellence because we are called to respond, in love, to the love of the Lord Jesus.

CHAPTER TWO

CONCEPTS OF EXCELLENCE

While on his history-changing military campaigns in Asia, Alexander the Great received disturbing news from his homeland. He was told that his mentor, the great philosopher Aristotle, had begun to teach publicly in Athens. Previously, Aristotle's insights had been reserved for a select group of students and Alexander was offended that such rare intellectual gems would become common knowledge. According to the historian Plutarch, Alexander took up his pen with indignation and wrote to his old teacher:

> Alexander to Aristotle, greeting. You have not done well to publish your books of oral doctrine; for what is there now that we excel others in, if those things which we have been particularly instructed in be laid open to all? For my part, I assure you, I had rather excel others in the knowledge of what is excellent, than in the extent of my power and dominion. Farewell.[1]

"The knowledge of what is excellent" is not simply a modern concern. In fact, the truth is quite the reverse. We tend to assume we understand what is meant by the term *excellent*, while ancient philosophers invested a great deal of attention to the subject. They correctly realized that the definition of *excellence* is not a problem of lexicography so much as of philosophy. The *Oxford English Dictionary* defines *excellence* as "the possession of good qualities in an eminent or unusual degree,"[2] a definition which tersely summarizes the word and exposes the problem. To speak of excellence is to speak about values; to address the question of what is "good." It goes beyond a consideration of skills and abilities to the question of worth and value. Ultimately, it raises questions about the nature and meaning of human life itself. As Conway has written:

> The idea of excellence is one shared by all civilizations; but the notions of what is the excellent, the best, vary over a wide range. In considering the concept of excellence in contemporary America, the temptation is to take for granted certain cultural and philosophical presuppositions inherent in our society and to measure excellence solely in terms of them. This would be an error, for it would get us no nearer to an understanding of what constitutes our notion of the best. We would not be discussing excellence but skill. *Excellence has to do with values and ideals rather than the expertness with which they are implemented.* It is the *summum bonum* of any culture at a given time. . . . What governs and in fact creates the idea of excellence in a society is its vision of reality, that which it considers to be true.[3]

Conway has identified the fundamental issue involved in the conception of excellence and has revealed a major reason for the absence of excellence observed by many contemporary social commentators. As Morrow accurately states, "Excellence demands standards. It does not usually flourish in the midst of rapid changes. This century's sheer velocity has subverted the principle of excellence."[4] Morrow accurately analyzed the problem, but blamed the wrong culprit. While the pace of social change has led to an erosion of standards, the main cause is moral and philosophical rather than technological. As Becker has observed, "There can hardly be any way of characterizing 'the good person' without reference to some logically prior notion of good per se."[5] The question of excellence inevitably involves a consideration of the standards required to evaluate what is good, and this leads to profound questions about the essential nature and purpose of human life.

A CALL TO EXCELLENCE

It is precisely at this point that modern society reveals its moral confusion. Because we have abandoned the concept of absolute divine standards, moral statements have been reduced to mere preferences. The result is moral statements which lack any real moral content. Obviously, a society which lacks any supreme values other than those of pluralism and moral relativism will find it almost impossible to rouse itself to the pursuit of excellence. What cannot be defined cannot readily be pursued!

Ethical humanists, with their man-centered philosophy, have an inevitable concern for the subject of excellence. As Rusterholtz pleads, "It is our duty and responsibility as human beings, and not mere animals, to devote ourselves to the pursuit of the good, the excellent, the best."[6] Yet his article is a pathetic lament that such is not the case in modern society. Two problems are evident. The first is the humanist's passionate commitment to human freedom, democracy, and equality. Striving for excellence seems to threaten equality, but the failure to strive produces mediocrity. Is it possible to have quality and equality? Gardner's book on excellence bears the subtitle, "Can We Be Equal and Excellent Too?" a query which has been called "perhaps the most serious question about democracy that we can raise."[7] The conflict between elitism and egalitarianism is of great concern to humanists, and their answer is found in an assumption that "potential excellence is universally distributed, but rarely actualized."[8] This unproven assertion is the basis of a call to excellence by which man completes himself and meets society's subjective ends. In fact, humanists believe that a culture is legitimate only as it permits individual excellence, for, as Nathanson claims, "The excellence of individual human beings is the supreme end and the chief meaning of both the democratic way of life and an ethical culture."[9] But this grand cathedral of humanistic excellence rests on an unprovable assumption about man.

The second major problem is the moral vacuum of humanism, as indicated by Becker:

We have reels of analysis on the fact-value distinction, the sources and nature of obligation, and the concept of moral responsibility. But comparatively detailed accounts—which go beyond the work of ancient philosophers—on the concepts of human excellence, on ideals, on the good person, are in notably short supply. . . . We are similarly ill-equipped to develop any sustained and illuminating accounts of standard of performance for moral conduct. Preoccupied with questions raised by attempts to decide what conducts are justifiable or required by duty, we have largely ignored the uneliminable question of what standards of performance are to be required. . . . We need criteria for deciding when someone has "done enough" to fulfill a given duty. Discussions of the problem are virtually nonexistent in philosophy.[10]

It becomes apparent that the consideration of the subject of excellence is intimately related to some fundamental questions about the nature of man and the purpose of life itself. Since the Word of God addresses those questions directly, it follows that there is a uniquely biblical view of excellence. Excellence is of supreme importance to the Christian, and there is a unique Christian perspective on excellence which is best understood by contrast with the major concepts of excellence which have been taught throughout history and which continue to be held in various forms. Five major schools of thought about excellence can be distinguished, and most of them, ancient in origin, have modern counterparts. When we speak of excellence, we are often unwittingly influenced by one of these perspectives. But each falls far short of excellence as God conceives it, and we will more clearly understand true excellence if we understand the inadequacies of various concepts of it.

PERSPECTIVES ON EXCELLENCE

SOCIAL EXCELLENCE. It is to the Greeks that we owe the most influential concepts of excellence, and it is Homer who first brought the idea into prominence with his notion of *arete*. He celebrated the heroic age of Greek society, a time which exalted the warrior and nobleman, and honored such qualities as military skill, courage, and loyalty. An excellent person was one who filled the vital roles of society. Because social contexts change, the content of excellence changes, but what is important is that it is described in social terms.

In modern terms, excellence is usually described as talents and achievements which are socially useful. Gardner, in his provocative call to excellence, is concerned about "the maximum development of individual potentialities at every level of ability" combined with "a commitment to the highest values of the society."[11] He summarizes his philosophy of excellence with an eloquent warning:

> But excellence implies more than competence. It implies a striving for the highest standards in every phase of life. We need individual excellence in all its forms—in every kind of creative endeavor, in political life, in education, in industry—in short, universally.
>
> Those who are most deeply devoted to a democratic society must be precisely the ones who insist upon excellence, who insist that free men are capable of the highest standards of performance, who insist that a free society can be a great society in the richest sense of that phrase. The idea for which this nation stands will not survive if the highest goal free men can set themselves is an amiable mediocrity. . . .
>
> Free men must set their own goals. There is no one to tell them what to do; they must do it for themselves. They must be quick to apprehend the kinds of effort and performance their society needs, and they must demand that kind of effort and performance of themselves and of their fellows. They must cherish what Whitehead called "the habitual vision of greatness." If they have the wisdom and courage to demand much of themselves—as individuals and as a society—they look forward to long-continued vitality. But a free society that is passive, inert, and preoccupied with its own diversions and comforts will not last long. And freedom won't save it.[12]

Gardner writes as a passionate and penetrating advocate of excellence, a man concerned for excellence as a necessity for social well-being. "Our society cannot achieve greatness unless individuals at many levels of ability accept the need for high standards within the limits possible for them."[13] The problem is that there is no ultimate basis for the values to which he appeals. If the standards for which men are exhorted to strive have no lasting significance, there is no compelling reason to seek excellence, particularly when a quest for individual fulfillment comes in conflict wih society's objectives. Gardner's appeal is rhetorical rather than real.

HUMAN EXCELLENCE. The most important and influential thinker on the subject of excellence was Aristotle. His concern was not with man in his social context, as was Homer's, but with man as man. His goal was to discover man's essential nature and the purpose of his existence. He taught that each creature and activity has a specific function and purpose, arising from its very nature. The excellence of a thing is related to the purpose for which it exists. Thus the excellence of a knife is that it cuts well and the excellence of a clock is that it tells time accurately. But what is the excellence of a man? Obviously it is related to the distinctly human purpose, but what is that purpose?

Aristotle's thought is too complex to relate in full here. Briefly, he contends that man's excellence lies in his uniquely human capacity for rational thought. The capacity to judge and to do the right thing, in the right way, at the right place, at the right time, is the essence of human excellence. It is important to grasp the central core of his thought. It is the *telos* (purpose or goal) of a man which determines where excellence lies. Since rationality is exclusively human, it is in the exercise of man's rational powers that an individual experiences human excellence and true happiness.

Aristotle's most important contribution is to define excellence in terms of man's *telos* or end. Unfortunately, he had a wrong concept of what that purpose is, and his scheme therefore falls. History makes it clear that reason cannot agree on a universally acceptable list of virtues and, as one commentator observes, "Aristotle would certainly not have admired Jesus Christ and he would have been horrified by St. Paul."[14] Most tragically, Aristotle's philosophy has no room for the redeeming work of Christ and the enabling power of the Holy Spirit. Human achievement is his pathway to excellence and there is no place for God's grace. "The story of the thief on the cross is unintelligible in Aristotelian terms."[15] A concept of excellence built apart from divine revelation and divine redemption is doomed to defeat.

PERSONAL EXCELLENCE. Aristotle's concern was for the excellence of man as a human being. However, his philosophy took a more personalized form in which "realize your humanness" came to mean "realize your individual potential and capacities." The sophists advocated one form of this doctrine, teaching that success is the goal of life, and virtue or excellence was whatever produced success. With such a concept, excellence became entirely relative, since success takes different forms in different contexts and requires different qualities at different times. Another form of the "self-realization" ethic interpreted Aristotle's concept of *telos* in purely personal terms. The unique abilities and gifts of an individual were taken as his personal means to excellence, so that excellence involved developing one's own, private self.

Modern psychology has made this concept of personal excellence pervasive in today's society. Terms such as "self-realization" and "self-actualization" have become contemporary buzz words. Self-help books exhort their readers: "feel good about yourself . . . love yourself . . . express yourself . . . assert yourself . . . realize your potential." However, as a concept of excellence, such slogans convey little meaning. Common sense indicates that the range of an individual's capacities are immense. There are many things an individual could do and many abilities he could develop, given adequate time and finances. How does one choose, since one must? Some capacities are possible but trivial. Should I actualize my potential as a Frisbee thrower or perhaps as a break dancer? As Hospers observes:

> We probaby have within ourselves the potentiality for painting over windows, eating snake-meat, preparing sandwiches containing sawdust, counting all the dandelions within a mile's radius of our residence, and barking like a dog for fifteen minutes each morning. But what point would there be in actualizing such potentialities? Even if there were, we could not in a thousand lifetimes actualize every potentiality we possess. If we actualize some of them, it must always be at the expense of most of the others. Besides, is it being suggested that we actualize our potentialities toward cruelty, sadism, deceitfulness, hypocrisy, pigheadedness, and asininity? These potentials are usually far easier to develop than their

opposites, yet it would be usual to maintain that we should try to discourage the development of these qualities. Clearly, then, some selectivity will have to be exercised in the matter of which potentialities to work on.[16]

The question of excellence unavoidably involves us in a discussion of values, and the slogan "Realize Your Potential" begs central questions. The question of the *telos* of human life is unavoidable. If an individual can develop only a certain range of capacities, how is that range chosen? Is the decision to be based on social custom, moral law, personal preference, or divine direction? Some capacities may be personally pleasing but also destructive, personally or socially. Furthermore, our "self-realization" might be gained only at the cost of direct harm to others. What is the relationship between excellence of character and excellence of achievement? None of these questions is merely theoretical, since this philosophy has left a destructive legacy of individualism gone rampant in modern life. "Self-actualization" too easily becomes self-absorption and self-indulgence. A view of excellence which is entirely egocentric fits comfortably into a narcissistic society such as ours, but it cannot provide a foundation for excellence.

The epitome of the personal ethic is Nietzsche. His contention was that all attempts to establish morality on an objective base have failed. There is therefore nothing to morality but expressions of will, and morality is only what the individual will chooses to create. Therefore, modern man, by a heroic act of the will, creates himself. The result is an aesthetic, rather than an ethical, standard for life. But Nietzsche's influence has been powerful. Because of the way he cut morality free from religious and traditional philosophical roots, MacIntyre calls him *"the* moral philosopher of the present age."[17]

MacIntyre mourns the influence of Nietzsche. Conway embraces it, while decrying his theories of "superman" and racial supremacy. He describes the effect of this on the contemporary view of excellence with an amorality that is chilling:

We evaluate and judge a man not on the basis of his moral life—how can we with so many differing ideas of what the correct moral life is?—but instead on the basis of his gifts and the skill and integrity with which those gifts are realized. We judge him on the completeness and line of the trajectory of his performance. This does not by any means exclude moral considerations. On the contrary. They are an important component but they have meaning only in so far as they affect the aesthetic totality. They are not primary. They derive their validity from their relation to the pattern of performance as a whole. The poor lawyer has no excellence either because he has no talent or because he has failed to fulfill it. The brilliant, dishonest lawyer fails in excellence because his performance constitutes an aesthetic affront. He does not present that harmony and unity and single-minded intellectual drive which his duty to his talent demands and merits. The observer experiences, not a moral shock in the old sense, but the shock, to borrow a particularly apt English expression, of bad form.

This subtle but profound shift in emphasis is probably best illustrated in the area of sexual mores. The impact of Freud's teaching has thrown our inherited convictions about sexual morality into confusion, with the result that, as a society, we have certainly no common belief about what is right or wrong in sexual matters. In the absence of belief about this and other moral concerns, we seek about for and have found another standard by which to judge people and their actions. Let me hasten to add that in my view this new standard is demanding. I am not suggesting a decline of the West or a collapse of our civilization. I do argue, however, that this change in fundamental standards has taken place. Private standards which continue the old traditional beliefs remain very strong. However, what is important is that they operate not in a congenial but in a neutral or hostile public atmosphere. More and more the law (as is evidenced by the decision here and in England to allow the publication of *Lady Chatterley's Lover*) reconciles itself with what, for lack of a better word, must be called an aesthetic standard of justification. We no longer agree about the good man and what to expect from him. We do, however, agree about the gifted man and what to expect from him. And this has become our point of departure. It explains our competitiveness and our achievements as well as our conformism and a good many of our neuroses.

What is most admired then, what constitutes our concept of excellence, is talent and its triumphant fulfillment. The kind of talent admired varies from level to level of literacy and cultivation. All levels have in common the concept of fulfillment, that is, success. The talent admired may be athletic (this runs through the whole range of our society) or literary or scholarly or artistic. It may be the capacity to compose music or play or conduct it or to write a novel or a poem or a distinguished work of scholarship. It may be the gift of the scientist or the doctor or the lawyer, or it may be the simple gift of making money. The point is that in a certain sense all these objects of admiration are the same. . . . They are all material goals.[18]

Such a view of excellence produces either the nihilism of a Nietzsche, the elitism of a Hitler, or the moral anarchy of modern society. Such a view is entirely self-defeating, for materialism breeds mediocrity and individualism provides no context in which excellence can be nourished.

UTILITARIAN EXCELLENCE. There is a pragmatic approach to the subject of excellence which defines it in terms of means to external ends. The goal may be happiness or material prosperity or public acclaim. However the goal is defined, excellence sustains a strictly utilitarian relationship to it. MacIntyre uses Benjamin Franklin as a symbol of this approach to moral virtue. His characterization effectively displays one form of utilitarianism, a view which obviously bears little resemblance to biblical teaching:

Franklin's account, like Aristotle's, is teleological; but unlike Aristotle's, it is utilitarian. According to Franklin in his *Autobiography*, the virtues are means to an end, but he envisages the means-ends relationship as external rather than internal. The end to which the cultivation of the virtues ministers is happiness, but happiness understood as success, prosperity in Philadelphia, and ultimately in heaven. The virtues are to be useful and Franklin's account continuously stresses utility as a criterion in individual cases: "Make no expense but to do good to others

A CALL TO EXCELLENCE

or yourself; i.e., waste nothing," "Speak not but what may benefit others or yourself. Avoid trifling conversation," and, as we have already seen, "Rarely use venery but for health or offspring. . . ." When Franklin was in Paris he was horrified by Parisian architecture: "Marble, porcelain, and gilt are squandered without utility."[19]

But such utilitarianism produces a shrunken view of life. Great literature or art will not flourish in such a context, and many of God's gifts will lie buried. What is commercially or pragmatically excellent rarely stands the test of time.

TECHNICAL EXCELLENCE. A fifth category of excellence focuses specifically on skills. Excellence in spheres such as athletics, the arts, and science primarily involves the application of skills to performances and activities. Each field of endeavor has unique skills, the performance of which at a high level can be said to constitute excellence. In most cases, character is not a primary factor. The moral life of a surgeon will have some bearing on his professional competence, but questions of character are usually seen as secondary, or altogether irrelevant.

Studies of excellence tend to cluster around three areas: leadership, education, and business. Yarmolinsky has contended that "the kind of excellence most explicitly recognized in the United States is leadership, and the reward of recognition is, by and large, more leadership."[20] Certainly, excellence in leadership is of major interest in all sectors of society. Excellence in education has become a national concern, inspiring presidential commissions and endless discussions. A major defect of the discussions is the assumption that increased pedagogical competence will transform the educational system. However, the value structure of society may be fostering an intellectual mediocrity which increased pedagogical competence, no matter how desirable, cannot reverse. Waterman and Peters have addressed the question of excellence in business in a provocative and very popular study of successful companies. Their definition of excellence is notably utilitarian. Excellence means innovation, and "innovative companies are especially adroit at continually responding to change of any sort in their environments. . . . The companies that seemed to us to have achieved that kind of innovative performance were the ones we labeled excellent companies."[21] These continuously innovative, large companies share many factors in common but the authors summarize their success in one, simple sentence: "The excellent companies were, above all, brilliant on the basics."[22]

There is much to be learned from the study of individual excellence. It deserves to be fostered and honored. But it lacks a goal and purpose beyond itself and results in segmented spheres of life. Therefore, it requires a larger framework, if it is to be truly meaningful. Excellence of achievement or performance is highly desirable. But it is tragic if it exists alone. Our society abounds with individuals admired for public excellence whose private lives are less than admirable.

THE BIBLICAL PERSPECTIVE ON EXCELLENCE

The various perspectives on excellence differ in a variety of ways. But they share in common an attempt to define excellence in purely human terms. Whether social role, human rationality, self-realization, utilitarian success, or technical competence, each concept is horizontal in focus. The concept of excellence is also sharply circumscribed in most cases. Aristotle came closest to a theory which combined excellence of character with excellence of activity, but his position is deeply flawed by his Athenian elitism and his truncated description of character. Each of the concepts also lives in the realm of comparison. Excellence involves superiority with respect to others. For Aristotle, a slave could never be excellent, no matter how exalted his character. For Nietzsche, the heroic superman alone is worthy of praise, and all lesser beings are viewed with contempt, especially if they are non-German. Those who achieve technical excellence measure themselves by others. The inevitable result is that it is not excellence that is achieved, so much as pride. As C.S. Lewis indicates:

> Pride is *essentially* competitive—is competitive by its very nature—while the other vices are competitive only, so to speak, by accident. Pride gets no pleasure out of having something, only out of having more of it than the next man. We say that people are proud of being rich, or clever, or good-looking, but they are not. They are proud of being richer, or cleverer, or better looking than others. If everyone else became equally rich, or clever, or good-looking, there would be nothing to be proud about. It is

the comparison that makes you proud: the pleasure of being above the rest. Once the element of competition has gone, pride has gone.[23]

The sin is not in competition per se, but in the pride which results from it or motivates it. Exactly the opposite result is possible—a sense of personal frustration which is demotivating and discouraging.

The biblical concept of excellence does not deny all that is found in the other models, but it sets the consideration of excellence into an entirely different context. The delineation of the unique, Christian perspective is the subject of the following chapters, but seven distinct features of that concept need to be set against the models previously considered.

1. There is *a different standard* of excellence—God. Biblical ethics is radically theocentric. Thus the character of God provides the point of comparison, and the result is humility. As Lewis observes:

In God you come up against something which is in every respect immeasurably superior to yourself. Unless you know God as that—and therefore, know yourself as nothing in comparison—you do not know God at all. As long as you are proud, you cannot know God. A proud man is always looking down on things and people; and, of course, as long as you are looking down, you cannot see something that is above you.[24]

2. There is *a different model* of excellence—Christ. The Lord Jesus is excellence personified for the believer. To live with excellence is to live as He lived.

3. There is *a different goal* of excellence—Christlikeness. Aristotle was correct in defining excellence in terms of the unique human *telos*. However, the uniqueness of man is not his intrinsic rationality, but his destiny of fellowshipping with God and partaking of the divine nature. The destiny of the believer directly affects our duty here and now. To paraphrase Aristotle, man's excellence is a progressive realization of his God-given purpose (*telos*) of Christlikeness. Since our destiny is conformity to the image of God's Son (Rom. 8:29), that goal must shape our present conduct.

4. There is *a different focus* of excellence—character. The Word of God places emphasis on achievements of excellence. But excellence of achievement only has lasting meaning as an extension of character. Excellence of talent is not the central concern of God in a believer's life, though it is certainly not to be demeaned, provided godly character balances it. What a person is gives meaning to all that he does.

5. There is *a different basis* of excellence—revealed truth. Excellence involves a statement of values, and this is the primary weakness of all other models of excellence. The values expressed are either arbitrary or relative. A model of excellence cannot long stand on a sandy foundation of relativistic values. In contrast, the Christian possesses an absolute and revealed value system, which provides the fixed substructure for a concept of excellence.

6. There is *a different motive* for excellence—God's glory. Excellence can be sought for a variety of reasons, both noble and ignoble. The unique Christian ambition is to please God and to walk worthy of Him. This is a powerful incentive, born out of the grace of God experienced by the believer. Allied closely to the motive of pleasing God is the motive of glorifying Him by revealing His character. This certainly requires a lifestyle of excellence.

7. There is *a different enablement* for excellence—grace. It has been contended by critics of the Gospel that it is the enemy of excellence because it "induces men to rely upon the grace of God instead of summoning them to human achievement."[25] The Bible clearly teaches the nonmeritorious nature of human works, but it is a distortion of the doctrine of grace to suggest that it produces passivity and human mediocrity. On the contrary, grace is the great incentive for Christian excellence as well as its enablement. The indwelling of the Spirit means that a believer is able to do what he otherwise could not, to the glory of God.

CHAPTER THREE

THE STANDARD OF EXCELLENCE

Hyman Rickover was a crusty old sailor who became a legend in the United States Navy. Known as the father of the nuclear navy, his most enduring legacy was his impact on the men who served under him, most notably a future president, Jimmy Carter. One Navy captain measured him with the following assessment: "Look around. Do you see excellence anywhere? In medicine? In law? Religion? Anywhere? We have abandoned excellence. But Rickover was a genius who gave a generation of naval officers the idea that excellence was the standard."[1]

We may quibble with the man's lament about the absence of excellence, but we understand his enthusiasm. It is exhilarating to be around people who embody excellence. Teachers, coaches, bosses, mentors, organizations—some stand out and leave an indelible impression. They inspire us to higher standards, challenge our complacency, make us dig deeper than we thought possible, and teach us that mediocrity is an enemy. For them, excellence is the standard, and because it was for them, it is for us as well.

But to set excellence as the standard is not enough. What is the standard of excellence? How do we identify and measure it? Because excellence involves values, it requires standards. The futility of man-centered concepts of excellence is that they demand values, but can provide nothing more than those which are relative and tentative. Furthermore, they offer no large vision which provides harmony and unity. A man who is "excellent" in business may sense no continuity with his family or social responsibilities. An athlete may be a public hero and a private failure. In such cases the very commitment to excellence that is applauded produces disintegration and conflict. To have value, excellence must be a concept which integrates all of life.

Standards are also essential to excellence because they provide necessary criteria to measure achievement. In their best-selling study of business, *In Search of Excellence*, Waterman and Peters return again and again to the theme of values and standards. For example, they report that "in most of the excellent companies, these basic values run deep"; that excellent companies are "fanatic centralists around the few core values they hold dear"; and that "every excellent company we studied is clear on what it stands for, and takes the process of value-shaping seriously." They are "driven by coherent value systems" and therefore "require and demand extraordinary performance from the average man."[2] In fact, they suggest that such companies have seven basic values:

1. A belief in being the "best"
2. A belief in the importance of the details of execution, the nuts and bolts of doing the job well
3. A belief in the importance of people as individuals
4. A belief in superior quality and service
5. A belief that most members of the organization should be innovators, and its corollary, the willingness to support failure
6. A belief in the importance of informality to enhance communication
7. Explicit belief in and recognition of the importance of economic growth and profits.[3]

Gardner also recognizes the critical role of values and standards. His concern is for social excellence, and he accurately portrays the contagious influence of standards:

Standards are contagious. They spread throughout an organization, a group, or a society. If an organization or group cherishes high standards, the behavior of individuals who enter it is inevitably influenced. Similarly, if slovenliness infects a society, it is not easy for any member of that society to remain uninfluenced in his own behavior. With that grim fact in mind, one is bound to look with apprehension on many segments of national life in which slovenliness has attacked like dry rot, eating away all the solid timber.[4]

But the question remains: if excellence is the standard, what is the standard of excellence? Anthropocentric ethics eagerly affirm the former, but have no satisfactory basis for the latter.

The biblical concept of excellence addresses the necessity of values and standards directly. Excellence can only be understood in light of the purpose of an activity or creature, and God alone determines the purpose of man. Thus, biblical excellence is radically theocentric. Its central question is not, "What can man become?" but "What does God intend?" The will of God thus becomes the harmonizing principle of excellence as well as the standard of evaluation. Four components unite to provide a comprehensive standard of excellence—the character of God, the creation of God, the calling of God, and the command of God. An understanding of each of these theocentric elements is foundational to a biblical concept of excellence, and 1 Peter 1:14-16 provides a very important framework:

> As obedient children, do not be conformed to the former lusts which were yours in your ignorance, but like the Holy One who called you, be holy yourselves also in all your behavior; because it is written, "You shall be holy, for I am holy."

THE CHARACTER OF GOD AND EXCELLENCE

Biblical excellence has its moorings in the character of God. The believer lives under the mandate, "You shall be holy, for I am holy" (Lev. 19:2; 1 Peter 1:16). The Lord Jesus' command is parallel: "Therefore you are to be perfect, as your Heavenly Father is perfect" (Matt. 5:48). The principle is awesome, but undeniable: *the Christian's standard of excellence is nothing less than the character of God.* Such a standard necessarily imposes humility on every believer, since it infinitely transcends the capacities of mortal man. But the fact that a standard is ultimately unreachable does not render it inoperative or meaningless. Indeed, it provides a high and holy incentive to move beyond a passive satisfaction with the status quo.

The holiness of God is the central truth of His person. It is not simply one of His attributes, but rather an affirmation of all that He is as God. The angelic beings celebrate His holiness in heaven (Isa. 6:3; Rev. 4:8), and forty times in the Old Testament He is described as "the Holy One." Holiness is thus the controlling characteristic of His character, His actions, and His relationships. All that He does is holy. He is, in the words of David, "righteous in all His ways" (Ps. 145:17); His love is holy love; His power is holy power; and His will is a holy will. Holiness is thus a comprehensive statement about God's person, rather than being one attribute among others.

For most of us, holiness is a difficult concept to understand. When my son Stephen was still a preschooler, we were traveling in the car when he introduced a statement with the exclamation, "Holy cow!" I took the opportunity to remind him that we, as a family, didn't use that expression, and tried to explain to him that only God and His things are holy. He nodded his four-year-old agreement, and finally concluded with the observation, "But you can say holy Scriptures, can't you, Dad, 'cause the Bible's God's Word?" I assured him he could, and on we drove, I happily convinced I had taught an important theological truth to my son. About ten minutes later came an excited shout, "Holy Scriptures, Dad—look over there!" The Lord gives us children to keep us humble! But many of us have an understanding of God's holiness only slightly more accurate than Stephen's.

The holiness of God is simply the excellence of His person which sets Him apart from His entire creation. The Old Testament term to describe God as holy conveys the idea of that which is set apart and separate. This is true in two ways. God possesses *majestic holiness*. That is, He is set apart from His creatures in His position. He is the Lord, "lofty and exalted" (Isa. 6:1), "the high and exalted One who lives . . . on a high and holy place" (Isa. 57:15), "majestic in holiness" (Ex. 15:11). He is thus transcendent and majestic. God also possesses *moral holiness*. He is set apart in His person from any imperfection or impurity. Thus God's holiness is His moral excellence, and the term describes the infinite perfection which characterizes Him. In this ethical sense, holiness is, as Berkhof states, "the perfection of God, in virture of which He eternally wills His own moral excellence, abhors sin, and demands purity in His moral creatures."[5]

The holiness of God is, as 1 Peter 1:14-16 indicates, the standard of excellence, and indeed of all moral behavior. As A.H. Strong observes, "According to the Scriptures, the ground of moral obligation is the holiness of God, or the moral perfection of the divine nature, conformity to which is the law of our being."[6] God does not conform to any standard outside Himself. In His holiness, He alone is that standard. This standard is not arbitrary. A.W. Tozer insightfully comments, "God is holy and He has made holiness the moral condition necessary to the health of His universe."[7]

The attributes of God are a compelling standard of excellence in and of themselves. But the central truth of the Christian faith is that "the Word became flesh, and dwelt among us" (John 1:14). In Him, excellence became incarnate, "for in Him [Christ] all the fullness of Deity dwells in bodily form" (Col. 2:9).

In all that the Lord Jesus did and was, excellence is manifested. God the Father publicly announced that He was well-pleased with Him (Matt. 3:17; 17:5). Describing His miracles and actions, the amazed crowds exclaimed, "He has done all things well" (Mark 7:37). When His enemies sent officials to arrest Him, they returned with the report, "Never did a man speak the way this Man speaks!" (John 7:46) Those who knew Him best and lived with Him intimately told their readers that He committed no sin (1 Peter 2:22), for "in Him there is no sin" (1 John 3:5; cf. Heb. 4:15; 2 Cor. 5:21). Because He is the exact representation of God's nature (Heb. 1:3), He perfectly expresses all that God is. Because He lived on earth as a true man, He is the perfect model of human excellence; He has left an example for believers to follow in His steps (1 Peter 2:21). Ramm expresses the role of the Lord Jesus as our model:

> Jesus Christ is everywhere in the New Testament assumed to be the moral and spiritual ideal of the Christian. In His purity of life, perfect obedience to the Father, composure in the hour of persecution, steadfastness in

suffering, and resistance to sin, He is the model for the Christian when he enters into similar situations. In this life, we strive to be like the Saviour; in our end-time glorification, our souls shall be perfectly conformed to His image.[8]

The New Testament emphasis in describing Christ is on who He is. What He did is of great value because of its congruence with His character. The miraculous deeds, the powerful words, the sacrificial death would all be meaningless apart from His sinless life and holy character. This concept of congruence between character and performance is of great importance to biblical excellence. Thus, the Lord Jesus provides both a model of excellence and a visible standard for excellence.

THE CALLING OF GOD AND EXCELLENCE

Peter is concerned in his first epistle not only to remind believers of who God is, but of who they are. In terms of the past, we were characterized by ignorance and indulgence ("the former lusts in your ignorance," 1 Peter 1:14). Life was desire-based, rather than obedience-based. But believers have come to the obedience of faith and therefore are "children of obedience," chosen for obedience to Christ (1:1-2) and purified by obedience (1:22). Obedience is therefore the entire atmosphere of Christian living, and therefore the Christian is called to holiness and obedience. Because we are called by a holy God, we are called to a holy life. Because we, as God's children, have heaven as our destiny, we must live by heavenly standards in this present world.

God's purpose in grace transcends man's loss through sin. The eternal plan of God is that God's elect people "become conformed to the image of His Son, that He [Jesus] might be the firstborn among many brethren" (Rom. 8:29). Christlikeness is thus the destiny of the believer, a destiny to be realized at the Rapture. The return of the Saviour means instant glorification for the Christian: "We know that when He appears, we shall be like Him, for we shall see Him as He is" (1 John 3:2, NIV).

Christlikeness means, first, that believers will possess a resurrection body like that of the Lord Jesus. He "will transform the body of our humble state into conformity with the

41

body of His glory" (Phil. 3:21). This is what Paul has in mind when he promises that "just as we have borne the image of the earthy, we shall also bear the image of the heavenly" (1 Cor. 15:49).

Christlikeness, however, means more than a bodily likeness to the risen Lord. John is speaking in a moral context when he suggests likeness to Christ (1 John 3:2-3), since the implication of this truth is that believers are to purify themselves. This moral transformation is also the emphasis in Colossians 3:9-10 (NIV): "Do not lie to each other, since you have taken off your old self with its practices and have put on the new self, which is being renewed in knowledge in the image of its Creator." It is evident that the Creator-creature distinction between the Lord and His people will never be erased, but it is also clear that glorification involves a fundamental change of human nature. Schep describes the transformation as follows:

> To live in such a world man need not be deprived of his body of flesh, in which resides the image of God, any more than Christ needed to abandon His body of flesh. What man needs is a change in the *conditions* of his body and of his *whole humanity*; a change from corruptibility, perishability, dishonor, and all that belongs to this earthbound life, to indestructibility, immortality, glory, and all that is characteristic of a world which indeed may be called heaven on earth, and where the Spirit of God fills man's body and soul to the brim, as He does the new Adam, the life-giving Spirit.[9]

The believer is thus destined for the time when "the perfect" comes, and all that is imperfect will be done away (1 Cor. 13:10). It is then that God's purpose for the believer will be achieved and justification will reach its goal. The believer in God's presence will be holy (Eph. 1:4), sincere (Phil. 1:10), and blameless (1 Cor. 1:8; Phil. 1:10; 1 Thes. 3:13). Conformity to Christ is therefore the announced purpose of God for the believer.

A fundamental New Testament principle is that destiny determines duty. Since Christlikeness is the believer's goal, believers are to move at present toward that goal. Though perfection awaits the Rapture, the Apostle Paul seeks to bring every man to a mature condition in Christ (Col. 1:28) and he himself pursues the same goal in his own life (Phil. 3:11-13). Because the believer's destiny is glorification, "everyone who has this hope fixed on Him purifies himself, just as He is pure" (1 John 3:3). Because Christlikeness is our destiny, increasing conformity to Christ is our desire and the direction of our lives.

A passage of fundamental importance in this regard is 2 Corinthians 3:18. The believer has a privilege unknown to Old Covenant believers, in that he is privileged to look on the glory of the Lord Jesus. As he does, he is gradually transformed from one degree of glory to another through the indwelling Holy Spirit. This change is neither instantaneous nor final. Only at the Rapture will the complete image of Christ be manifested in the believer. But the process of progressive sanctification means that the Holy Spirit is gradually producing Christ's image in each believer's life.

THE COMMAND OF GOD AND EXCELLENCE

Peter's words also point to a third standard of excellence. God's character of holiness and God's calling of the believer to holiness are accompanied by His clear, unequivocal command of holiness. "Like the Holy One who called you"—this establishes the standard of holiness. "Be holy yourselves also in all your behavior"—this delineates the extent of holiness. "Be holy, for I am holy"—this indicates the reason for holiness. Overarching all is the undeniable responsibility for holiness. God has commanded believers to live with moral excellence in an immoral and unholy world.

The call to holiness is not new. In fact, the command is repeated four times in the Holiness Code of Leviticus (11:44-45; 19:2; 20:7, 26). The contexts of those commands are well worth studying. Areas as diverse as food, worship, sexual conduct, care for the poor, fairness to employees, honesty, and love are seen as expressions of holiness. The central idea was that Israel was a people distinct among the nations, since it was set apart to God. Its national life was molded not by its external neighbors or its internal desires, but rather by the declared will of God. Holiness affected all that the people were and did—from the food they ate to the rituals they practiced to the relationships they established. And when they were obedient to God's calling, they were free to achieve God's purpose. For Israel, holiness meant excellence, the realization of God's goal for them as a nation. In that way, holiness was both healthiness and happiness.

The nature of holiness for the New Testament believer is similar. Every area of life is to reflect the glory of God. Holiness is a command, not an option. It does not come by passively waiting for God to give it, but by actively obeying God in dependence on the Holy Spirit. It involves the disciplined forming of holy habits. Clearly, however, the definition of holiness has changed. The standard is no longer rules and regulations given at Sinai, but the revelation of excellence found in the person of the Lord Jesus. We also live under the blessing of the New Covenant, which means that every believer enjoys the indwelling power of the Holy Spirit. But the command is unequivocal in its consistency. A believer must be holy in character. He lives under the imperative of excellence because that is the character and command of the God who has called him to share His life and holiness. Robert Murray McCheyne caught the essence of the biblical attitude when he prayed, "Lord, make me as holy as it is possible for a saved sinner to be." He understood that true excellence begins not in our achievements or our ministries, but in our character. Writing as a pastor, he wrote, "My people's greatest need is my personal holiness." It is tempting to complete that sentence in another way. Surely our churches need excellence of preaching or excellence of administration. But above all, they require excellence in holiness. The same is true for every Christian, whatever his or her sphere of life. Holiness is God's priority.

THE CREATION OF GOD AND EXCELLENCE

There is a fourth standard which is not mentioned in 1 Peter 1:14-16, but which is essential to a proper biblical concept of excellence. Excellence is grounded in the fact not only that God is who He is, but that man is who he is. God's purpose for man is revealed in His creation of him. By virtue of our original creation in the image of man, we have been vested with natural talents. This means that each individual possesses a rich but often untapped variety of gifts and abilities. The believer has also experienced regeneration and becomes a new creature in Christ. Because of this new creation, we possess

44

spiritual gifts through the indwelling Holy Spirit.

COMMON GRACE AND NATURAL TALENTS. "Then God said, 'Let Us make man in Our image, according to Our likeness. . . .' And God created man in His own image, in the image of God He created him" (Gen. 1:26-27). The exact meaning of the image of God has aroused considerable discussion and debate among theologians. Most probably the term involves a complex of ideas, related to all that links man to God and distinguishes him from other earthly creatures. Of central importance is the recognition that "God was the original of which man was made a copy."[10]

Because of man's fall into sin, the image of God is marred but not lost, as Genesis 9:6, James 3:9, and 1 Corinthians 11:7 indicate. Therefore, the psalmist can celebrate the skill and wisdom of God displayed in the human body:

> For You created my inmost being; You knit me together in my mother's womb. I praise You because I am fearfully and wonderfully made; Your works are wonderful, I know that full well. My frame was not hidden from You when I was made in the secret place. When I was woven together in the depths of the earth, Your eyes saw my unformed body. All the days ordained for me were written in Your book before one of them came to be (Ps. 139:13-16, NIV).

David is celebrating the fact that the human body displays the excellence of God's omniscience, omnipotence, and omnipresence. God's skill is displayed even in the embryo. Therefore, every individual, by virtue of divine creation and common grace to fallen man, possesses gifts and talents.

Any ability possessed by man is ultimately a gift of God. We are therefore responsible to God for the use of our talents. Our abilities to act, to achieve, to invent, to perform are all manifestations of God's rich provision for us. However, these abilities reflect the purpose of God for men and are to be used consistently with His purpose. The tower of Babel is eloquent testimony that human skills used for purely human goals without regard for God's will are a perversion of God's provision (Gen. 11:1-9). Human excellence involves the development of human abilities under divine direction.

SPECIAL GRACE AND SPIRITUAL GIFTS. The believer in Christ possesses not only natural talents, but spiritual gifts. The distinct nature of the two is evident from the fact that natural gifts are possessed from birth and are common to all men, while spiritual gifts are the possession of believers alone (cf. 1 Cor. 12:7, 11; Rom. 12:6; Eph. 4:7; 1 Peter 4:10). A spiritual gift is best defined as "an enablement which the Lord Jesus gives through His Spirit to every believer to enable him to serve God in some specific way."[11] These gifts are sovereignly given by the Head of the church through the Spirit (Eph. 4:7-8; 1 Cor. 12:11) for the edification of the body (1 Cor. 12:7).

Spiritual gifts are given in rich diversity to God's people. The truth of the physical body's unity, diversity, and interdependence is used by Paul as a rich illustration of the way God provides individuals and the church with gifts (Rom. 12:3-8; 1 Cor. 12:12-31). No believer is insignificant or self-sufficient. Indeed, it is only as believers individually serve one another at the point of their gifts that the body of believers comes to maturity in Christ (Eph. 4:11-16). The ultimate purpose of the gifts is "that in all things God may be glorified through Jesus Christ" (1 Peter 4:11).

Spiritual gifts are thus God's further provision to believers. He has richly provided His people, by virtue of their natural talents and spiritual gifts, with all the resources for excellence. Clearly, excellence takes many forms, since every individual possesses a unique mix of talents, abilities, experiences, and circumstances. This individuality indicates that God's general purpose for man is allied to His specific purpose for each individual. But it must be recognized that excellence is only possible because of God's gracious provision of natural talents and spiritual gifts. Given by Him, they must be given back to Him and used for His glory.

The standard of excellence, in all its dimensions, is God Himself. Only a God-centered life can truly reflect excellence. In 1840, Robert Murray McCheyne wrote a letter to his friend Dan Edwards, who was preparing for missionary work among the Jews. His words speak of success in Christian ministry, but go far beyond to touch a basic principle of excellence:

I trust you will have a pleasant and profitable time in Germany. I know you will apply hard to German; but do not forget the culture of the inner man—I mean of the heart. How diligently the cavalry officer keeps his sabre clean and sharp; every stain he rubs off with the greatest care. Remember you are God's sword, His instrument—I trust a chosen vessel unto Him to bear His name. In great measure, according to the purity and perfections of the instrument, will be the success. It is not great talents God blesses so much as great likeness to Jesus. A holy minister is an awful weapon in the hand of God.[12]

Excellence is possible only because God has given us natural abilities and spiritual gifts. Excellence is measurable only with reference to God Himself as the standard of excellence. Excellence is indispensable, because a living God has commanded His people to be holy as He is holy. Excellence is possible only because God has committed Himself to making us like the Lord Jesus Christ, both ultimately and progressively. It is therefore obvious that true excellence requires a radically theocentric view of life, in which not only is excellence the standard, but the standard of excellence is God Himself. Such a perspective must have a transforming effect on every area of a Christian's life.

CHAPTER FOUR

AMBITIOUS FOR EXCELLENCE

Two Old Testament characters provide a fascinating study in contrasts. The first is Baruch, secretary and companion of the Prophet Jeremiah. He was a gifted man who came from a high-placed family, the grandson of a former governor of Jerusalem (2 Chron. 34:8), and the brother of one of King Zedekiah's chief officials (Jer. 51:59). Such family connections made it natural for Baruch to harbor political ambitions for himself. Or perhaps his admiration of Jeremiah caused him to desire a position of spiritual importance, perhaps as the prophet's successor. Whatever the precise reasons, Baruch possessed powerful ambitions, and therefore Jeremiah's predictions of inevitable judgment on the nation Judah came as a cruel blow. God's prophecy meant the ruination of Baruch's hopes. Realizing the inner turmoil of Jeremiah's associate, the Lord addressed a direct message to him through the prophet: "But you, are you seeking great things for yourself? Do not seek them" (Jer. 45:5).

Those reproving words have often been understood as a rebuke, not only of Baruch's ambition, but of all human ambition. It is not difficult to understand such a blanket condemnation. After all, it was the "I will make myself like the Most High" of Satan which brought sin into existence (Isa. 14:14) and Eve's ambition to be "like God, knowing good and evil" (Gen. 3:5) which brought sin into the world. The history of humanity provides eloquent testimony that human ambition is very often an agent of destruction, violence, and cruelty. Untrammeled ambition is often a species of madness.

However, God's message to Baruch is not all that Scripture has to say on the subject of ambition. Buried amid the genealogies of 1 Chronicles is the brief description of a man who is marked by the biblical writer as "more honorable than his brothers." Little is revealed about Jabez except one brief prayer he uttered and the witness of God's response to it found in 1 Chronicles 4:10:

> Now Jabez called on the God of Israel, saying, "Oh that Thou wouldst bless me indeed, and enlarge my border, and that Thy hand might be with me, and that Thou wouldst keep me from harm, that it may not pain me!" And God granted him what he requested.

Jabez was obviously a man of ambition, yet his ambition is approved by God. And this is not an unparalleled idea. The Apostle Paul writes of elders, "If anyone sets his heart on being an overseer, he desires a noble task" (1 Tim. 3:1, NIV). The recognition that there are unworthy and dishonorable ambitions must not obscure the importance of worthy and honorable ambitions. Indeed, the Lord Jesus often appeals to the ambition for heavenly rewards as an incentive to holy living (e.g., Matt. 6:1, 6, 18).

Ambition and motivation are of central importance to the subject of biblical excellence. Without ambition, mediocrity is inevitable. By virtue of creation and new creation, every believer is divinely equipped for excellence in a unique way. The difference between believers is not a matter of innate capacities so much as a question of motivation and ambition. For example, Ginzburg and Herma studied intellectually gifted young men who did superior work in graduate school. At that point in these men's careers, there was basic equality, but the years revealed a wide disparity in the degree of success achieved by each. No one factor accounted for this diversity, but motivation was a primary consideration. As Ginzburg and Herma conclude:

> What people achieve in their work and career depends in substantial measure on their motivation, attitudes, and

values. Other things being equal, those who seek to achieve the most will in fact achieve more than those who are less inclined to invest as much in their work and in the pursuit of their careers.[1]

There is nothing startling about such a conclusion. It is the expectation of common sense. Gardner similarly notes the results of a study by Terman and Cox. Having studied three hundred geniuses who made a mark on history, they concluded that such people "were characterized not only by very high intelligence but by the desire to excel, by perseverance in the face of obstacles, by zeal in the exercise of their gifts."[2]

However, recognition of the necessity of ambition does not dispel a Christian's uneasiness about it. Selfish ambition must be rejected, but there must always be a striving toward meaningful goals. The tension is ineradicable. There must be a constant evaluation of the ambitions fueling an individual's life. The diagnostic question, "If I got to where I am going, where would I be?" is a helpful, analytical tool. The question is nontheoretical, since it reveals what is ultimately shaping a person's life.

At the same time, it is dangerous to constantly analyze one's personal motivations. Such an attitude of introspection can result in a paralysis of analysis, and no individual's ambitions will ever be entirely pure. It is far more helpful to focus on those motivations which are appropriate for the believer and which will impel him to strive for excellence. To be meaningful, such motivations must be powerful enough to incite an individual to action and large enough to integrate the varied aspects of life, all in a central thrust toward the realization of God's purpose.

In 1 Peter 2:9-12, the apostle addresses words to his readers which delineate, in broad strokes, the three main ambitions or motivations to spiritual excellence which ought to shape the life of every believer:

But you are a chosen race, a royal priesthood, a holy nation, a people for God's own possession, that you may proclaim the excellencies of Him who has called you out of darkness into His marvelous light; for you once were not a people, but now you are the people of God; you had not received mercy, but now you have received mercy.

Beloved, I urge you as aliens and strangers to abstain from fleshly lusts, which wage war against the soul. Keep your behavior excellent among the Gentiles, so that in the thing in which they slander you as evildoers, they may on account of your good deeds, as they observe them, glorify God in the day of visitation.

These verses indicate that a Christian's life is to be shaped by three great ambitions which combine to produce a life of excellence. The Christian lives with a determination to *please God* by fulfilling His goal in his life, to *praise God* by revealing God's glory through his life, and to *proclaim God* by sharing God's Gospel through his life. John Henry Jowett, the great English preacher, spoke about the subject of ambition in words which bear careful consideration:

It is possible to evade a multitude of sorrows by the cultivation of an insignificant life. Indeed, if a man's ambition is to avoid the troubles of life, the recipe is simple: shed your ambitions in every direction, cut the wings of every soaring purpose, and seek a little life with the fewest contacts and relations. If you want to get through the world with the smallest trouble, you must reduce yourself to the smallest compass. Tiny souls can dodge through life; bigger souls are blocked on every side. As soon as a man begins to enlarge his life, his resistances are multiplied. Let a man remove his petty selfish purposes and enthrone Christ, and his sufferings will be increased on every side.[3]

THE MOTIVATION OF GOD'S GOAL

As we have seen, a fundamental principle of biblical ethics is that destiny determines duty. A parallel idea is that our position in Christ determines our practice in daily life. This is the doctrine which leads Peter to describe God's calling of the church. In words borrowed from the Old Testament, he calls us "a chosen race, a royal priesthood, a holy nation, a people for God's own possession" (1 Peter 2:9). The language is borrowed from Isaiah 43:20-21 and Exodus 19:5-6. Israel had a

51

special function in the world in an older dispensation which has now been transferred to the church. Peter does not equate Israel and the church nor do his words imply that the church permanently replaces Israel. He does, however, indicate that they have a similar mission in the world. God has given His people, by His grace, a position of great dignity and significance.

In stressing the position of Christians, Peter draws special attention to the fact that God has made us His people. Three terms express this. The church is a chosen race, called out from the nations. We are also a holy nation, a nation not as Israel was, but a distinct cluster of humanity set apart by God. Believers are also "a people for God's own possession." Behind the expression is a word which describes a valued property, a special treasure. In 1 Chronicles 29:3, the Hebrew word describes the treasure of gold and silver David accumulated for building the temple. Thus the church is God's special treasure on earth, valued and cared for by Him. Not long ago, my wife walked into the house, her face ashen. I immediately was concerned that she had had a car accident but through her sobs, she poured out her problem. The diamond was gone from her engagement ring. Over the next few days, she scoured our home and car and retraced her steps through stores and other buildings, hoping to find something which had special meaning, not so much for its intrinsic value as for its personal significance. She never did find the diamond, but it planted in our minds a vivid reminder of the immense value the Father places on the church of His Son.

Peter also indicates that the church is a royal priesthood. As Bigg suggests, "The priesthood is royal because it belongs to the King, who has chosen it as His own possession, and because, therefore, it shares in His glory."[4] As "royal," we share Christ's victory and eternally reign with Him. As a priesthood, we share Christ's ministry. The church has no priestly caste to mediate between God and men, but is itself a priesthood, representing God to men and men to God. The royal priesthood has a corporate ministry of worship, intercession, and service.

Furthermore, believers are God's showcase of grace. Peter borrows the language of Hosea 2:23 to remind us that we owe our position entirely to grace. Therefore, "those who formerly were not a people now are the people of God; those who had not been shown mercy now have received mercy."

The significance of this position must not be overlooked. The terms Peter uses do not describe a static position but a dynamic process. Thus believers are chosen, but election includes glorification. The royal priesthood will one day reign with Christ on the earth (Rev. 1:6; 5:10); the holy nation will enjoy final sanctification; the people who belong to God will one day be with Him. In this way, statements of position are also statements of divine purpose. They reflect God's goal for believers as well as His present gift of a position in grace.

The purpose of God for His people lies at the very heart of excellence. Since God's purpose is to make believers a distinct people who bear His image, the ambitions of a Christian must be consistent with this desire. God's goal requires that believers increasingly seek to manifest Christ's character in every area of their lives. Talents are given neither for self-glorification nor for self-realization, but as a means of manifesting Christ and revealing Him to others. When spiritual gifts and natural talents come to fruition, an individual is moving toward God's goal for every believer.

In the 1924 Olympics, in a feat celebrated by the powerful motion picture, *Chariots of Fire*, two Englishmen won gold medals. Their achievements were very similar, but their ambitions were very different. Harold Abrahams ran to command the respect of an establishment he found hostile to his Jewishness. Eric Liddel ran as a Christian, running to win but moved by a desire to please his Lord who had given him his formidable talents and to realize His purpose in every area of life. For Liddel, this was not an isolated occasion, but a pattern of life which later led him to serve as a missionary in China and finally to lay down his life serving others in a Japanese prisoner-of-war camp during World War II. His was true excellence— not only an outstanding achievement, but an entire pattern of life.

Excellence is not so much an achievable destination as a direction of life. Believers are people in process who move steadily onward in the pursuit of excellence. In such a process, goals are essential. Gardner writes from a secular perspective when he describes the necessity of goals, but his perspective harmonizes with that of Scripture:

We fall into the error of thinking that happiness necessarily involves ease, diversion, tranquility—a state in which all of one's wishes are satisfied. For most people, happiness is not to be found in this vegetative state but in *striving toward meaningful goals*. The dedicated person has not achieved all of his goals. His life is the endless pursuit of goals, some of them unattainable. . . .

We want meaning in our lives. When we raise our sights, strive for excellence, dedicate ourselves to the highest goals of our society, we are enrolling in an ancient and meaningful cause—the age-long struggle of man to realize the best that is in him. Man reaching toward the most exalted goals he can conceive, man striving impatiently and restlessly for excellence has achieved great religious insights, created great works of art, penetrated secrets of the universe, and set standards of conduct which give meaning to the phrase, "the dignity of man."[5]

There is no more meaningful goal than realizing God's purpose for one's life. To sense that God has gifted me in a unique way and has determined to transform me into the likeness of Christ is a powerful incentive to strive for excellence.

The motive for such striving is gratitude, a desire to please God. A Christian is not motivated on a deficit basis. Excellence of achievement ought not be a means of attacking a personal sense of insignificance or insecurity. Rather, we have received grace in Christ and stand complete in Him. Therefore, the believer is motivated by love rather than pride, by gratitude rather than anxiety. Such love makes the believer anxious to fulfill the Lord's purpose in his life lest, when the Lord appears, he is caused to shrink away in shame (1 John 2:28), knowing that he has disappointed the Saviour.

It is interesting that the Greek term for *excellence* is derived from the same root as the word meaning "to please." There is a strong link between spiritual excellence and a desire to please God. The Lord Jesus always did what was pleasing to the Father (John 8:29). At the same time, He did not live selfishly, to please Himself (Rom. 15:3). His life was entirely determined by the will of God for Him, and in doing that will, He found pleasure (John 4:34; 5:30; 6:38) and pleased God.

The concept of pleasing God is especially important for the Apostle Paul. Indeed, it was the goal and controlling ambition of his life, for, as he writes to the church in Corinth, "We make it our goal to please Him, whether we are at home in the body or away from it" (2 Cor. 5:9, NIV). Only a believer indwelt by the Spirit can please God, for "those who are in the flesh cannot please God" (Rom. 8:8). A further prerequisite is faith, for "without faith it is impossible to please Him [God]" (Heb. 11:6). The ambition to please God determines a person's commitment of life (Rom. 12:1; 2 Tim. 2:4), his daily walk (Col. 1:10; 1 Thes. 4:1), his spiritual priesthood (Heb. 13:15-16), and his relationships (Col. 3:20). The believer tests everything in life, "trying to learn what is pleasing to the Lord" (Eph. 5:10). A man who lives to please people by making their approval of more importance than God's stands condemned (Gal. 1:10), as does an individual determined to please only himself, regardless of the impact on others (Rom. 15:1-3).

The desire to lay hold of God's purpose of increasing conformity to Christ so that the Lord may be pleased is the very heart of biblical excellence. The Christian is anxious to "walk in a manner worthy of the Lord, to please Him in all respects" (Col. 1:10). The goal of life is not maximum personal satisfaction nor personal peace and affluence, but rather the satisfaction of God with the believer as His purpose is increasingly realized. This was the driving force of the Apostle Paul. As Hughes comments on 2 Corinthians 5:9:

> That is his consuming ambition, the motive force behind all that he does. To be well-pleasing to Christ is, indeed, the sum of all ambition which is truly Christian. In arresting contrast to the ambition of the world, it is centered, not on self, but on the Saviour; its goal is to please Him.[6]

THE MOTIVATION OF GOD'S GLORY

God's goal for His people is indicated by the position which He has given them and for which He is preparing them. It is a position with a very specific purpose, indicated by Peter's statement, "You are a chosen race . . . that you may proclaim the excellencies of Him who has called you out of darkness into His marvelous light" (1 Peter 2:9). Peter once again borrows Old Testament language, in this case, Isaiah 43:21, to express a profound truth for Christians. The central purpose of all Christian living is to glorify God and to reveal His character.

The glory of God is one of the great themes of Scripture. The Hebrew word *glory* is derived from a root with the basic meaning "to be heavy, weighty." The glory of an individual is that which gives him substance; that which gives him weight or importance in the eyes of others. For example, Abraham is described as "very rich [heavy] in livestock, in silver and gold" (Gen. 13:2). By extension, "to glorify" someone is to recognize his importance or to enable others to recognize that an individual is worthy of respect by helping them to recognize his true character.

The Greek word for *glory* originally described someone's opinion ("what I think") and also came to mean one's reputation ("what others think of me"). In this sense, an individual's glory is his fame and honor. Thus the Lord Jesus says to the Jewish leaders, "I do not accept praise [glory] from men. . . . How can you believe if you receive praise [glory] from one another, yet make no effort to obtain the praise [glory] that comes from the only God?" (John 5:41, 44, NIV) One's glory is one's reputation. But in the New Testament, "glory" also points to the substance which stands behind the praise. God's glory is not just His reputation, but His revealed character, the display of His attributes. To glorify someone therefore is to increase his reputation by revealing his true nature.

The two Testaments thus indicate that to glorify God is to live in such a way that His character is displayed and His praise is increased. To live in this way is radically different from the value system of the world. "For the Greeks, fame and glory were among the most important values in life. The rabbis also had a high esteem for a man's honor."[7] In contrast, the Christian lives to receive God's honor in heaven and to promote God's honor on earth. The highest duty and the highest privilege of man is to glorify God, and this obviously requires excellence of life. When Peter says that believers "proclaim the excellencies of Him who called you," he uses a term which suggests that Christians are living commercials, advertising the character of God. A Christian who realizes that he is a display case of God's glory will have an itching ambition to glorify the Saviour.

David Brainerd was a young man who gave himself in the early eighteenth century as a missionary to Indians in New England. He was a deeply spiritual man whom the Lord used to influence many in following generations through his journal. But tuberculosis ravaged his body, and two weeks before his death at the tender age of twenty-nine, he called his friends to his bedside. His words reveal the heartbeat of a man who still represents excellence centuries later:

> My heaven is to please God, and glorify Him, and to give all to Him, and to be wholly devoted to His glory. That is the heaven I long for; that is my religion and that is my happiness. . . . I do not go to heaven to be advanced, but to give honor to God. . . . All my desire is to glorify God. . . . I see nothing else in the world that can yield any satisfaction besides living to God, pleasing Him, and doing His whole will.[8]

Brainerd's life was short on quantity, but long on quality, because he was a man gripped by the greatest truth of life—that it is given to be used to glorify God.

The New Testament teaches that God has bound up His glory with the believer. Our bodies are temples of the Holy Spirit (1 Cor. 6:19-20), a phrase recalling the glory of God resident in the tabernacle and temple. In the present dispensation, the primary channel of His glory to the world is the church. This, in itself, is enough to establish the glory of God as the chief concern and central ambition of every believer. God's intention is that the entire plan of redemption accrue "to the praise of His glory" (Eph. 1:6, 12, 14).

That the Christian is to glorify God is clear. How he glorifies God is also a matter of divine revelation, and some important principles are given:

1. God is glorified when believers fulfill God's will for their lives. The Lord Jesus indicates this principle, recorded in John 17:4: "I have glorified Thee on the earth, having accomplished the work which Thou hast given Me to do." The Lord Jesus did not do all that He might have done. He was a relatively young man whose public ministry was brief and whose geographical constraint was extreme. Millions remained unreached, untaught, and unhealed. But He glorified God be-

cause He had completed 100 percent of the will of God for His life.

2. Any God-given responsibility or sphere of life is an area through which God may be glorified. "Whether, then, you eat or drink or whatever you do, do all to the glory of God" (1 Cor. 10:31) prohibits the division of life into sacred and secular realms where God may and may not be glorified.

3. God is glorified in the manner of our acting, whatever the sphere of our acting. What we do is to be done "in the name of the Lord" (Col. 3:17). Whatever the task, it is to be done "for the glory of the Lord Himself" (2 Cor. 8:19). Thus the glory of God is the central ambition of a believer, whether he is eating (1 Cor. 10:31), dealing with his sexuality (1 Cor. 6:18-20), working (Titus 2:10), praying (John 14:13), praising (Ps. 50:23), sharing the Gospel (2 Cor. 4:15; 2 Thes. 3:1), or maintaining unity among believers (John 17:22; Rom. 15:6). There are no specifically "sacred" categories of life in which God may be glorified in contrast to the profane spheres of life. Every area of life ought to be an arena of His glory.

4. God is glorified primarily through the character of a believer abiding in Christ. "By this is My Father glorified, that you bear much fruit, and so prove to be My disciples" (John 15:8). Fruit-bearing is the inevitable result of abiding in the Vine, and in the context of John 15, must refer to the visible product of Christ's life within the believer. As Christlikeness is produced, God is glorified and others are helped.

5. God's glory is inseparable from the welfare of His people. The life that glorifies God is not individualistic or isolated from fellow-believers (Rom. 15:5-6).

THE MOTIVATION OF GOD'S GOSPEL

A third motivation arises from Peter's exhortation and is closely related to the other two. The ambition of God's goal in the believer's life inspires him to excellence out of a desire to please his Creator and Redeemer. The ambition of God's glory challenges the believer to reveal God's character in every area of his character and actions, so that others might be taught to exalt Him. A third ambition relates the believer to the world. God's desire is to reach lost people, and thus Peter exhorts believers to "keep your behavior excellent among the Gentiles, so that in the thing in which they slander you as evildoers, they may on account of your good deeds, as they observe them, glorify God in the day of visitation" (1 Peter 2:12).

Peter's thought revolves around the mandate of evangelism. Christians are a unique people in the world. As sojourners and strangers, we possess values and a citizenship alien to the world. Our time here is only temporary. During my seminary years in Dallas, I was in the United States as a resident alien. There is very little difference between Canadians and Americans, and for most of the year, I rarely thought about my status as a "sojourner and stranger." But isolated events and the requirement to register with the government once a year reminded me of who I really was. Much as I enjoyed the States, it was not my homeland nor was its value system entirely the same as mine. But my status also involved a responsibility. For many Americans, I was one of the few Canadians they had ever met and what they thought of Canada was largely determined by what they thought of me.

Peter's thought is similar. As believers, we belong elsewhere, but we have responsibilities in this world. As aliens, we are ambassadors of Christ, and what others know of the eternal homeland, God's eternal city, will be learned through us. Therefore, we must not derive our values from the present world or from the ever-present "fleshly lusts which wage war against the soul." To be conformed to the world is to betray our heavenly citizenship and, therefore, Christians must live an attractive, beautiful, excellent lifestyle. We are to "keep [our] behavior excellent among the Gentiles," not so that it will be easier to live in a hostile environment, but so that others will see the reality of Jesus Christ in our lives and glorify Him also.

The life of the Christian ought to give eloquent testimony to the reality of the Gospel. A life of excellence gives plausibility to the truth of the message. Peter is insisting that what Christians say and are should match. Almost certainly, Peter had in mind the words of the Lord Jesus, recorded in Matthew 5:13-16:

You are the salt of the earth; but if the salt has become tasteless, how will it be made salty again? It is good for nothing anymore, except to be thrown out and trampled underfoot by men. You are the light of the world. A city set on a hill cannot be hidden. Nor do men light a lamp, and put it under the peck-measure, but on the lampstand; and it gives light to all who are in the house. Let your light shine before men in such a way that they may see your good works, and glorify your Father who is in heaven.

Christ's Parable of the Tares focuses on the good seed sown by the Lord in the field of the world. The description and identity of the seed is significant. "As for the good [excellent] seed, these are the sons of the kingdom" (Matt. 13:38). The Lord's strategy of evangelism involves sowing a certain kind of man, an excellent person, in the world. Excellence is essential to evangelism because God works by the power of attraction. The life we possess from God must be the life we express in the world.

When Charles Spurgeon was a young man, he had a great desire to enter college to prepare more thoroughly for the ministry. But an interview with the school's president went astray because of a servant girl's mistake. That afternoon, as the seventeen-year-old Spurgeon walked to preach at a country mission, he sensed the Lord speaking to him in unmistakable terms, in the Lord's words to Baruch: "Seekest thou great things for yourself? Seek them not." Those words penetrated deep. "This led me to look at my position from another point of view, and to challenge my motives and intentions."[9] Deep thoughts for a seventeen-year-old, but God honored Spurgeon's ambition to serve Him, regardless of what the future held by way of fame or obscurity.

It is not enough to be highly motivated. A wise person is motivated by high motives. There are no higher motives than those which focus on God and propel a believer to excellence. Therefore, a Christian who seeks excellence is committed to the purpose of God, the person of God, and the program of God. These combine to form a harmonious, unified thrust to life. Not all that can be done by a person should be done. Therefore, a believer must evaluate individual activities and responsibilities in view of these three transcendent motivations. Together, they provide a God-centered focus which informs and transforms every part of life. Most of all, they focus on character. In each case, what a person is has precedence over what he does. God's goal is to conform the believer to Christ. God's glory is entrusted into the limitations of human character. His Gospel must be seen or it will not be heard.

Excellence, therefore, is demanded by these three biblical ambitions. Striving for excellence is the essence of Christian living. Gardner has captured the necessity of such striving in memorable terms:

> Though we must make enormous concessions to individual differences in aptitude, we may properly expect that every form of education be such as to stretch the individual to the utmost of his potentialities. And we must expect each student to strive for excellence in terms of the kind of excellence that is within his reach. Here again we must recognize that there may be excellence or shoddiness in every line of human endeavor. We must learn to honor excellence (indeed to *demand* it) in every socially accepted human activity, however humble the activity, and to scorn shoddiness, however exalted the activity. As I said in another connection: "An excellent plumber is infinitely more admirable than an incompetent philosopher. The society which scorns excellence in plumbing because plumbing is a humble activity and tolerates shoddiness in philosophy because it is an exalted activity will have neither good plumbing nor good philosophy. Neither its pipes nor its theories will hold water."[10]

For the Christian, more is at stake than pipes or theories! The reputation of God Himself, the destinies of others, and the fulfillment of God's purposes for him are involved in the excellence he seeks.

CHAPTER FIVE

THE FOCUS OF EXCELLENCE

The record for the shortest major league baseball career probably belongs to a member of the old Brooklyn Dodgers, a pitcher named Harry Hartman. He was a gifted young ballplayer whose day of glory arrived in 1918 when he was called up from the minors to pitch against the Pittsburgh Pirates. This was the moment he'd dreamed about, the beginning of a great career, but his dreams began to fade when his first pitch was hit for a single. The next batter tripled. Rattled, he walked the next batter on four straight pitches, and when he did throw a strike to the next hitter, it went for a single. At that point, Hartman had had enough. He headed for the showers, dressed, and walked out of the stadium to a naval recruiting office, where he enlisted. The next day, he was in a military uniform, never to be heard from in professional baseball again.[1]

There is nothing more discouraging than the feeling that you don't measure up, that you don't have what it takes and are therefore destined for mediocrity. Discussions about excellence can have the same effect, since they almost inevitably become considerations of accomplishments and achievements. Our society values "doers," and therefore the excellence we admire is the scientist's brilliant discovery, the musician's remarkable performance, or the athlete's record-breaking victory. But few of us can realistically aspire to such activities. On the personal level, we tend to evaluate people by what they do, instinctively categorizing them by their occupations, talents, visible achievements, or material possessions. Even in churches, people who receive approval are most often those with communication skills, musical abilities, or organizational talents. We persist in seeing excellence in terms of what people do.

Excellence of achievement is an important contribution to the quality of life. However, if excellence is primarily a matter of superior talents, then most of us are foreordained to mediocrity, and excellence is reduced to a spectator sport in which an excellent elite performs while the multitude observes. Far too often, precisely that has taken place. Most Christians have opted out of the pursuit of excellence, feeling that they are not gifted for the race. Others live under the burden of unrealistic expectations. Harassed by the endless problem of priorities, they are immobilized or demoralized. If value is determined primarily by what one does, how does a person find his niche, and what if he can't compete?

The Word of God neither minimizes nor negates excellence of achievement. However, Scripture consistently insists that excellence is preeminently a character term. Excellence of achievement has value when it is the extension of character, and no person will take his God-given gifts, talents, and opportunities more seriously than a believer who is growing progressively toward Christlikeness. But a Christian begins at the center of life, not on the circumference. Excellence of character has a priority over excellence of achievement. This priority has an important bearing on the establishment of priorities in daily living. Priorities are notoriously difficult to establish. We seem to live in a crossfire of competing demands and conflicting values. Therefore, a wise person ponders deeply the principles which will guide his choices and enable him to do things in order of importance. It is important to see that a central biblical priority is our own selves, not in the sense of indulging our desires, but rather developing our characters. Paul's admonition to Timothy establishes an important order: "Pay close attention to yourself and to your teaching" (1 Tim. 4:16).

The modern world tends to define excellence as achievement and pays little attention to the question of character. We are encouraged to jump on life's speeding treadmill, even if the direction and destination seem unclear. The Word of God values excellence of achievement, but only when it is an *extension* of excellence of character. Even excellence of character is not an end in itself, since it produces a life which is both practically useful and divinely approved. Second Peter 1:2-11 describes the relationship between these areas, making it very clear that *character development is the key to spiritual usefulness:*

> Grace and peace be multiplied to you in the knowledge of God and of Jesus our Lord; seeing that His divine power has granted to us everything pertaining to life and godliness, through the true knowledge of Him who called us by His own glory and excellence. For by these He has granted to us His precious and magnificent promises, in order that by them you might become partakers of the divine nature, having escaped the corruption that is in the world by lust.
>
> Now for this very reason also, applying all diligence, in your faith supply moral excellence, and in your moral excellence, knowledge; and in your knowledge, self-control, and in your self-control, perseverance, and in your perseverance, godliness; and in your godliness, brotherly kindness, and in your brotherly kindness, love. For if these qualities are yours and are increasing, they render you neither useless nor unfruitful in the true knowledge of our Lord Jesus Christ. For he who lacks these qualities is blind or shortsighted, having forgotten his purification from his former sins.
>
> Therefore, brethren, be all the more diligent to make certain about His calling and choosing you; for as long as you practice these things, you will never stumble; for in this way the entrance into the eternal kingdom of our Lord and Saviour Jesus Christ will be abundantly supplied to you.

The flow of Peter's thought is readily detectable. Having described God's resources for a godly character in verses 3-4, he turns to describe the believer's responsibility in verses 5-7. His primary emphasis is on the process of Christian character development, as believers move toward Christlikeness. A godly character results in spiritual usefulness, and so Peter concludes the paragraph by describing the spiritual benefits which accrue to an excellent character. The message of verses 8-11 is of great importance since it declares unequivocally that excellence of character is the key to spiritual usefulness and divine approval. As Henry Martyn once wrote, "Let me be taught that the first great business on earth is the sanctification of my own soul."

GOD'S RESOURCES FOR GODLY CHARACTER

Godly character is possible because God, in His grace, has made adequate provision for the believer. Our resources are not a result of our attainments, but God's free gift, indicated by the repetition of the word *granted* in 2 Peter 1:3-4. Both verses use the past tense, indicating that these resources are part of the believer's birthright; divine gifts which become ours the instant we enter God's family. The two resources, then, are the provision of His divine power (v. 3) and the provision of His divine promises (v. 4).

By virtue of union with Christ and the presence of the indwelling Holy Spirit, believers have received God's power in unlimited measure. When a believer comes to the Lord Jesus in faith and trust, he not only receives the gift of eternal life, but is also given the privilege of entering into personal fellowship with God Himself. As the Lord Jesus prayed, "This is eternal life, that they may know Thee, the only true God, and Jesus Christ whom Thou hast sent" (John 17:3). That is Peter's thought here. Salvation consists of nothing less than "the true knowledge of Him who called us by His own glory and excellence." The Lord Jesus is the One who called us to salvation by opening our eyes to the glory of His divine person and the excellence of His human life. When we realize that He is exactly the Saviour we need, our hearts are opened by the Holy Spirit to faith in Him.

But Peter's emphasis is that our knowledge of the Lord Jesus brings power from Him. In other words, the Christian life operates on the contact principle. Let me explain, using examples from the world of transportation. An automobile works on the reservoir principle. As long as it has gas in the tank, it operates independently of its source of supply. But an electric train operates on the contact principle. It has power only while it remains in contact with its electrical source, but that contact is a source more than adequate for all its needs.

Christian living follows the second pattern. We cannot operate independently of the Lord and experience His enablement. His divine power brings its blessings "through the true knowledge of Him."

Peter wants us to realize that God's provision is totally adequate for all of life's demands. He has granted us "everything pertaining to life and godliness." As Hudson Taylor once wrote, "God's power is available power. We are supernatural people, born again by supernatural birth, kept by a supernatural power, sustained by supernatural food, taught by a supernatural Teacher from a supernatural Book. We are led by a supernatural Captain in right paths to assured victories. The risen Saviour, ere He ascended on high, said, 'All power is given unto Me. Go ye therefore.' " That supernatural power, however, operates in a very profane world. It is the enablement which relates to "life," not only eternal life, but life as it is lived in this world for God. It is a power which makes "godliness" possible: holy living in an unholy world. It is impossible to think of a more comprehensive phrase than "everything pertaining to life and godliness." Peter wants us to realize that we cannot claim that moral excellence is beyond our capacities. Unaided, it undeniably is. But the divine provision overflows human inadequacy, a divine provision which must be appropriated to become operative.

The second great provision for the believer is the divine promises. God's power is allied to His purposes for us, revealed in "His precious and magnificent promises." Such promises look forward to all that God has determined to do for the believer, especially the time when the Lord Jesus returns for His people (2 Peter 3:4) and establishes a "new heavens and a new earth, in which righteousness dwells" (3:13). As Peter wrote, he was very conscious that the time of his death was near (1:14), and, as death drew closer, the promises of God shone even brighter. Those promises focused on the Lord Himself, His coming glory, and the great certainty that believers would be "partaker[s] also of the glory that is to be revealed" (1 Peter 5:1).

Wordsworth once lamented that "the world is too much with us." Our perspectives and our values are shaped by the realities of the present age; thus we constantly need to be reminded that we are eternal people, bound for an eternal destiny. The fallen world is subject to corruption. Nothing on earth escapes the fact that man's fall into sin has meant that "the creation was subjected to futility," laboring under "its slavery to corruption" (Rom. 8:20-21). The word *corruption* usually implies physical, rather than moral, corruption in the Scriptures (e.g., 1 Cor. 15:42, KJV), and Peter is reminding us that sin has brought into being the cycle of decay, death, and disintegration which so thoroughly dominates our modern world. But God's promise contains the good news that, at the Rapture, we will escape such corruption and at last share God's immortality. The bodies of our humiliation will be transformed into conformity with the body of His glory (Phil. 3:21) and in that way, we will become partakers of the divine nature, entering into the "inheritance which is imperishable and undefiled and will not fade away, reserved in heaven for [us]" (1 Peter 1:4).

Back in 1730, John Wesley read these verses, was touched by them, and a few days later reported in his journal: "Through all these days, I scarce remember to have opened the New Testament but upon some great and precious promise, and I saw more than ever that the Gospel is in truth one great promise."

Promise is indeed woven into the very fabric of the Gospel, but why does Peter focus on it here? First of all, he wants to remind us of our destiny, that moral transformation into Christlikeness which is God's future for us. Second, he wants to remind us that we will fully enjoy God's inheritance only when we are set free from bondage to corruption and lust. Holiness is a prerequisite for ultimate wholeness. Third, he wants us to realize that God's promise contains a present pattern of life. There is a sense in which our ultimate destiny of fellowship in the divine nature begins now. The divine promises which describe our destiny are also incentives to escape the corrupting influence of lust now and to seek increasing conformity to Christ. Thus Peter writes, "Therefore, beloved, since you look for these things, be diligent to be found by Him in peace, spotless and blameless" (2 Peter 3:14). The purpose of God's promises is to prepare us for the future by giving a deeper sense of the importance of character development, while the purpose of God's power is to provide the enablement for a godly life.

THE BELIEVER'S RESPONSIBILITY
FOR A GODLY CHARACTER

Having described the divine provision, Peter now delineates the responsibility of believers. Excellence of character is possible because of God's provision, but it is not automatic. The Christian must engage in a rigorous process of character development, a process which involves a fundamental attitude combined with a pattern of development. It is not enough to rejoice in the blessings of 2 Peter 1:3-4. Logic indicates that such provisions require a practical response, and "for this very reason," we are to take action, "applying all diligence."

The word *applying* suggests the first of three prerequisites for growth Peter gives. The word literally means "to bring in alongside." In other words, a human response needs to be brought in alongside the divine provision. God's grace is basic to Christian growth, but human effort is not eliminated. It is most important to maintain a biblical balance. Rigorous self-effort is not the way to godly character, but neither is passivity. Human effort is inadequate for excellence, but it is also indispensable. Apart from Christ, a believer cannot bear fruit (John 15:5). Yet our lives must be disciplined toward God's goals. The first prerequisite for growth is a sense of *responsibility* for our condition. It is tempting to leave character growth to God or to accept the verdict of certain schools of psychology that we are the prisoners of our past. God's call, however, is for us to apply ourselves.

The second attitude conveyed by Peter is *intensity*. We are to apply "all diligence." The phrase describes a determined eagerness to carry out a task, a sense of moral earnestness and zeal. Excellence does not come to the halfhearted or apathetic. The Greeks saw diligence as an essential quality of the good man who was seriously aiming at excellence. No one who was complacent could be a truly good man. The New Testament also depicts diligence as an essential quality for Christian living, whether in maintaining unity (Eph. 4:3), meeting needs (2 Cor. 8:7, 16-17), exercising leadership (Rom. 12:8), or seeking God's approval (2 Tim. 2:15). Thus, Christians are never to lack zeal (Rom. 12:11). Intensity and diligence are indispensable to excellence. On the other hand, sluggishness, indifference, and complacency have no place in the life of the growing Christian. A teacher of long standing complained vehemently when he was passed over for an administrative promotion. "I've had twenty-five years' experience." "No, Sir," came the forthright reply. "You've had one year of experience repeated twenty-five times." Peter is exhorting us not to coast with the momentum of past achievements.

The third attitude conveyed by Peter is that of *abundance*, indicated by the word translated *supply*. The word originally described a Greek citizen who acted as a public benefactor by paying the expenses of a chorus in staging a play. Such an act involved considerable expense, but because it was a means of public esteem, such patrons tried to outdo one another in the equipment and training they provided. The word thus came to depict a lavish and generous provision. By using the term, Peter emphasizes the need of believers to carry on the task of character development with enthusiasm. A Christian is not to aim at the bare necessities. He ought to cooperate with his God with energy and abundance.

Peter's attitude is therefore exactly parallel to Paul's. In Paul's mind, believers are not merely to "walk and please God." They are, rather, to "excel still more" (1 Thes. 4:1). Excellence of character will not be realized by casual people. Nor is godly character the inevitable product of time. Only the determined and the disciplined develop excellence.

Having established the prerequisites for growth, Peter now sets forth its pattern, a list of seven character qualities which are to be present in the Christian's life. It is significant that he does not ask us to supply faith, but "in your faith supply." Every Christian possesses faith as the means to new life, and it is also the foundation stone of godly character. In fact, none of the character traits will be possible apart from a vigorous faith in the Lord Jesus.

The character sketch Peter gives is a beautiful portrait of the mature Christian. In fact, there is little difference between this portrait and Paul's portrait of the Spirit-filled man (Gal. 5:22-23). None of the virtues are dispensable, and Peter makes it clear that each quality is interlocked with the others. It should also be evident that such qualities are not built into a life in a linear manner. We do not add one quality after another. Rather, we grow in all these areas progressively. Each quality is required and must be supplied, but the degrees of development will differ, and none is ever present in its fullness. In other words, Peter wants us to realize that character development is a dynamic and complex process, which is never-ending for the believer.

The qualities which Peter describes are fascinating and provide a powerful basis for personal character analysis. The first to be supplied is *moral excellence*, the excellence which he ascribed to Christ in 2 Peter 1:3. Faith which does not produce Christlikeness is mere orthodoxy. But excellence must be enriched by *knowledge*, the knowledge of God, which produces practical wisdom and moral discernment. There can be no excellence in ignorance. The mature Christian life also displays *self-control*, the mastery of one's impulses. Self-control involves all of life and ultimately comes through believing submission to the control of the indwelling Christ. Self-control enables a believer to deal with his impulses, while another virtue, *perseverance*, describes the endurance which sustains an individual under sorrows and difficulties and which enables him to keep pressing on with his eye fixed beyond present problems. But Christian character is more than stoic endurance. It involves *godliness*, a worshipful attitude to God which shapes daily life. To be godly is to be properly related to both God and man. It also displays *brotherly kindness:* love for fellow believers, displayed in acts of kindness. The crown jewel of Christian character is *love*, the sacrificial love displayed supremely in the Lord Jesus, which is the greatest of all virtues and without which everything else is useless (1 Cor. 13:1-3, 13). Love for our brothers is important, but God's desire goes even further. He wants us to become loving people.

THE PRACTICAL RESULTS
OF CHARACTER DEVELOPMENT

Excellence of character is given biblical priority, not to demean excellence of achievement, but to make it possible. Technical competence apart from moral quality inevitably produces moral anarchy or moral corruption, a process evident in modern society. Excellence of achievement must be directed toward worthwhile goals and guided by moral principles. Modern society reflects the futility and danger of scientific excellence in a context of emotivism and utilitarianism. Competence without character makes the very skills one possesses tools to serve demonic ends. In strictly utilitarian terms, Satan's works are marked by "excellence." All that he does takes place with the highest level of skill and competence. Satanic skill is, however, directed by satanic character to satanic ends.

Peter emphasizes the value of spiritual excellence in terms of its results. When it is present in a believer's life, it provides spiritual usefulness (2 Peter 1:8-9), promotes spiritual confidence (v. 10), and produces spiritual approval (v. 11).

SPIRITUAL USEFULNESS. A barren, unfruitful life is the very opposite of excellence. Therefore, Peter's promise is encouraging: "If these qualities are yours and increasing, they render you neither useless nor unfruitful" (2 Peter 1:8). The term *increasing* is important. Peter is describing a process rather than an event or status. The essential question is whether or not the believer is growing. How far we have gone is not nearly as determinative as which direction we are going. A believer who is increasing in Christlike character will enjoy a life which is bold, useful, and fruitful. It is striking that the sphere of growth is the same as the blessing of salvation, "the true knowledge of our Lord Jesus Christ" (1:8). Fellowship with the Lord Jesus is both the beginning and the goal of the Christian life.

However, strong words are used to describe a person who lacks these qualities. He is *useless*, a word literally meaning "not working" and therefore sterile and ineffective. He is also unfruitful and unproductive. Changing the illustration, he is "so shortsighted as to be blind." As a person troubled by poor eyesight, I can identify with Peter's illustration. If I misplace my glasses, suddenly everything becomes fuzzy and unfocused. I lose perspective, so that it becomes dangerous to drive, and I lose the ability to see things at a distance. My judgment is suspect because I can't process the information I need. In the same way, a man with defective moral character suffers from defective moral and spiritual vision. He cannot see life clearly and even the most self-evident issues lose their focus. What we are affects what we see and what we see certainly determines what we do. Furthermore, such a person suffers from spiritual amnesia, "having forgotten his purification from his former sins." He has become forgetful of his true identity as a forgiven sinner in Christ and continues to live as if the old man still existed. Clearly, for such a man, excellence is impossible.

71

SPIRITUAL CONFIDENCE. A second blessing of godly character is that it provides a certification of one's election. Election is not something that lies within the power of men. God graciously has chosen some to salvation, an election which is both pretemporal and unconditional (1 Peter 1:1-2). It would be entirely foreign to the New Testament to suggest that a believer's life in any way secures his calling or election. These believers, who already enjoy the divine election, are to be diligent to make it sure. The word Peter uses is a legal term which described the confirmation of a sale and the guarantee which went with it. Thus, God-given miracles attest the truth of the apostles' message (Heb. 2:3-4) and the Transfiguration made the prophecies of the Lord's return "more sure" (2 Peter 1:19). As God's Word, the prophetic word is absolutely certain and trustworthy, but the Transfiguration confirmed it by grounding it in a historical event. In one sense, a believer cannot make God's election more certain than it already is, for it is grounded on His sovereign purpose. But the believer can provide living confirmation of his position in Christ by his growth in grace. In this way, his election is grounded in life, so that the reality of God's work of salvation is attested by a godly character. Healthy spiritual growth thus brings a deepened personal assurance about the Lord's work of salvation.

Together with the confirmation of salvation comes the confidence of perseverance, "for as long as you practice these things, you will never stumble (2 Peter 1:10). This does not mean that a believer will never sin, but it does suggest that there will be no irretrievable failure in a Christian's life. The promise is of continued growth in maturity and godliness, a spiritual surefootedness in one's walk through life.

SPIRITUAL APPROVAL. The third result indicated by Peter is divine approval. "In this way the entrance into the eternal kingdom of our Lord and Saviour Jesus Christ will be abundantly supplied to you" (2 Peter 1:11). Not only will such a believer enter heaven, he will enter it richly. His welcome will be rich and full. Entrance into heaven is not on the basis of godly character but through regeneration (John 3:5). However, an abundant entrance is God's special provision for the spiritually mature. Peter may have in mind an honor accorded to a victor in the Olympic games. The champion would not only receive a wreath, but also a special civic celebration. His home city would not allow him to use the city gate, but would break a special entrance in the wall through which he would enter. That kind of abundant entrance is a prelude to the believer's reception by God. Spiritual excellence not only leads to usefulness on earth but to approval in heaven.

Durham relates an event which provides an interesting parallel to the picture Peter gives here. He writes:

What will it be like to reach heaven? A story out of the recent past may give us some idea. During June, July, and August of 1965, an ordinary man from Cleveland, Ohio lived out a dream. Forty-six-year-old Robert Manry purchased a thirteen-and-one-half foot, thirty-year-old, dilapidated boat. He repaired her, christened her *Tinkerbelle*, and learned to sail. Then on June 1, 1965 his dream began. He set out from Falmouth, Massachusetts for Falmouth, England, far across the Atlantic.

Manry's voyage was to take seventy-eight days, many of them cold, wet, and painful. Hit by storms, confused by hallucinations of hitchhikers and assassins, washed overboard, delayed by winds that were too great and becalmed by lack of wind at all, plagued by loneliness, and troubled by saltwater sores, he kept sailing.

Manry expected to sail into Falmouth Harbor quietly, let his family know of his arrival, secure passage for himself and *Tinkerbelle*, and return to the States. It did not turn out quite that way. Word of his voyage had reached England. As he neared the coast, Shackleton bombers from the R.A.F.'s 42nd squadron flew over in salute. Newspaper teams from both sides of the Atlantic vied for his story. Great ships hovered alongside with congratulatory messages.

During the last miles, a flotilla of ships and boats sailed out of Falmouth to greet him. Royal Navy helicopters formed an umbrella above. Boats circled and flocked about him and the people called out, "Good show!" "Glad you made it, Mate!" "Well done, well done!" Sailing along the quay, he could see crowds of cheering people jamming the ramparts of Pendennis Castle. Manry later wrote:

"People were everywhere; standing along the

shore, perched on window ledges, leaning out of door-ways, crowded onto jetties, thronging the streets, cling-ing to trees, and cramming the inner harbor in boats of every size and description. The whole place was teeming with humanity. I heard later that 50,000 people were there to see *Tinkerbelle* and me complete our voyage.

I was dumbfounded, numbed by the enormity of it all, and not a little bewildered. It was just too much to take in all at once . . . every boat and ship in the harbor let go with its horn or whistle and shook the whole wa-terfront with reverberating sound as the crowd yelled. R.A.F. Shackletons flew overhead in wigwagging salutes and a band . . . St. Stythian's Silver Band, played 'The Star-Spangled Banner' and 'The Stars and Stripes Forever.' "[2]

This is the prospect awaiting the believer who is charac-terized by the moral qualities Peter describes in 2 Peter 1:5-7. Such a life will outlast earth and thus will be truly excellent. It is interesting to note that the process comes full cycle. The believer is to supply these virtues richly to his life. When he does, God reciprocates with the promise that He will richly supply a welcome in heaven for us, and His standards are far more generous than ours. He will lavishly equip heaven for us and us for heaven.

It is impossible to miss the message of 2 Peter 1:3-11. Character development is the key to usefulness. Therefore, excellence of character rather than excellence of achievement must be the central concern of the believer. However, a believ-er's character is not in a special compartment, isolated from the rest of life. The priority of character is due to the fact that what a person is colors all that he does. There is a direct correlation between usefulness and excellence.

If character is the Christian's priority, this has great im-portance in an activity-centered culture. What a man is is more important than what he does. But character is not developed instantly or in isolation. Character is forged in the crucible of life's experiences only by the most diligent application of effort on the believer's part and by his constant dependence on the provision and promises of God. The qualities which Peter de-scribes as part of the mature believer's character require him to confront difficulty and suffering and call him to be involved in the lives of other people.

At the same time, character development requires a carefully maintained private life. Paul emphasizes the believer's need to let his mind dwell on those things consistent with the character of Christ. "Finally, brethren, whatever is true, whatever is honorable, whatever is right, whatever is pure, whatever is lovely, whatever is of good repute, if there is any excellence and if anything worthy of praise, let your mind dwell on these things" (Phil. 4:8). An excellent character requires the careful cultivation of all that is consistent with conformity to Christlikeness and the rigorous elimination of all that is contrary to it. It is neither easily nor immediately achieved, but remains as God's priority for the believer. The consistent teaching of the Word is that true excellence is grown and not conferred in immediate response to even the most earnest prayer.

CHAPTER SIX

THE PRACTICE OF EXCELLENCE

One night in late summer, I turned on my television hoping to see a Dallas Cowboys' football game. Instead, I found myself transfixed by one of the most powerful programs I have ever seen. It was a report on the International Special Olympics, a sports event that brought together more than 4,000 athletes from forty-three countries. I was moved by the courage of young men and women battling against difficulties and discouragements which would have sidelined others. I was humbled by their determination to participate which made it irrelevant whether they won or lost. I was overwhelmed by their emotions which contained some of the purest displays of joy I have ever seen. Even now, recalling those scenes, I am moved to tears by the sheer beauty of their efforts.

No records were set in that stadium which might threaten the great athletes of our time. No columns were devoted to the event on the nation's sports pages. Yet the slogan of the games, "A World of Winners," was undeniably demonstrated. And it raises some inescapable questions about the nature of excellence. A badly crippled girl finished seventh in a race of seven runners, but each step was a battle with pain. Was she any less excellent than the woman who stands atop the victory podium at the Olympic games? The young man, handicapped by brain damage as an infant, completed his gymnastics routine with a clumsy grace which gave lie to all the therapists who said he could never walk. Though he would never be allowed in a regular competition, can any word other than *excellent* be applied to his performance?

Excellence has an absolute standard: the character of God Himself. But it also has a relative dimension which derives from the fact that the focus of the biblical concept is the personal character of the believer. The believer's ultimate destiny is to be conformed to the character of Christ, and such a destiny establishes a responsibility to increasingly display His character in daily living. This inevitably leads to excellence of achievement and performance. Talents, skills, and spiritual gifts are all expressions of the image of God within believers and come under the mandate of excellence. Doing things well ought to be the inevitable result of living well, since talents and gifts are the means by which God may be glorified. But God has not given each believer the same gifts or capacities. My responsibility is not to become what someone else is, but to become the best that I can be under the sovereign hand of God.

Excellence is not confined to a few limited spheres of life. Our God has chosen to people His world with individuals possessing a vast array of talents and abilities. Further, He has set before us a cornucopia of opportunities and activities. Some are utilitarian and meet practical human needs. Others are enriching, texturing human life with beauty and harmony. Gifts of both scientific endeavor and cultural expression come from God and reflect something of His character. Excellence is only possible because of God's creation. And excellence is desirable in every sphere of life. For the Christian, the greatest motivation to excellence is not just that it is pragmatically useful, but that it is an act of doxology or praise. As the Apostle Paul so simply puts it, "Whatever you do, do all to the glory of God" (1 Cor. 10:31).

In every area of his life and activities, the Christian serves as a representative of Christ. This is true whether we are using our natural talents in the world or exercising our spiritual gifts in the church. Since all these capacities are God-given, they are divine stewardships for which we are accountable to Him. The nature of this stewardship is the theme of the Lord's Parable of the Talents, recorded in Matthew 25:14-30. It is a passage of great importance in establishing a biblical attitude toward gifts and capabilities.

For it is just like a man about to go on a journey, who called his own slaves, and entrusted his possessions to them. And to one he gave five talents, to another, two, and to another, one, each according to his own ability; and he went on his journey.

Immediately, the one who had received the five talents went and traded with them, and gained five more talents. In the same manner the one who had received the two talents gained two more. But he who received the one talent went away and dug in the ground, and hid his master's money. Now after a long time the master of those slaves came and settled accounts with them. And the one who had received the five talents came up and brought five more talents, saying, "Master, you entrusted five talents to me; see, I have gained five more talents." His master said to him, "Well done, good and faithful slave; you were faithful with a few things, I will put you in charge of many things, enter into the joy of your master." The one also who had received the two talents came up and said, "Master, you entrusted to me two talents; see, I have gained two more talents." His master said to him, "Well done, good and faithful slave; you were faithful with a few things, I will put you in charge of many things; enter into the joy of your master."

And the one also who had received the one talent came up and said, "Master, I knew you to be a hard man, reaping where you did not sow, and gathering where you scattered no seed. And I was afraid, and went away and hid your talent in the ground; see, you have what is yours." But his master answered and said to him, "You wicked, lazy slave, you knew that I reap where I did not sow, and gather where I scattered no seed. Then you ought to have put my money in the bank, and on my arrival I would have received my money back with interest. Therefore take away the talent from him, and give it to the one who has the ten talents." For to everyone who has shall more be given, and he shall have an abundance; but from the one who does not have, even what he does have shall be taken away. And cast out the worthless slave into the outer darkness; in that place there shall be weeping and gnashing of teeth.

The context of the parable is of central importance to its interpretation. The Lord's Olivet Discourse begins with a description of the Lord's return (Matt. 24:3-31), as the Saviour responds to the disciples' double question, "When shall these things be, and what will be the sign of Your coming, and of the end of the age?" (24:3) Implicit within the truth of the Lord's imminent return is the fact of His impending absence. He will depart before He returns. If, then, the Lord is to be absent, what is the disciples' responsibility in the interim? To answer that question, the Lord uses a series of parables, each of which describes His sudden return and its implications for His servants. The Lord's consistent emphasis is on the need for watchfulness and vigilance. A wise servant is one who is waiting and prepared for the Master's return. More than that, he is working while he waits. The unique contribution of the Parable of the Talents is to emphasize this last idea. *The time of waiting is a time of working and this working involves faithfulness to the stewardship given by the departed Lord.*

It should also be observed that the Lord's parable refers, in its original setting, primarily to the Jewish people in the future Tribulation period. As a nation, they have been entrusted by God with responsibilities for which He will hold them accountable. This primary reference is important for understanding some aspects of the parable, but it does not prevent applying the Lord's words to present-day believers. We also have been entrusted by God with "talents," which we are to use while our Lord is absent and until He returns.

THE ENTRUSTMENT OF THE MASTER

Tourists who visit Monticello in Virginia are impressed not only with owner Thomas Jefferson's inventiveness, but also the luxuriant lifestyle he enjoyed in the late eighteenth century. The Lord's parable centers on a similarly wealthy estate owner of the first century, a man of riches and importance, who found it necessary or desirable to take a lengthy journey away from his home. In so doing, he decided to entrust partial responsibility for his affairs to three of his servants, one of whom was to administer five "talents," another two "talents," and a third, one "talent." The word *talent* is rather misleading, since the Greek word *talanton* did not refer to an ability but to a unit of weight, and then to a unit of coinage. It is always difficult to translate ancient monetary values into our modern world, but the most useful method is to recognize that one talent contained 6,000 denarii. Since a denarius represented a day's wage for a common laborer, a talent involved almost twenty years' wages, an amount approximating half a million dollars in modern terms! The estate owner had, therefore, given to each of his servants a considerable responsibility. Nonetheless, it is important to recognize that, while this treasure was entrusted to each of the servants, it was a stewardship, not a gift. They were to use it for the master, not for themselves.

These details are not merely background coloring, but express three important truths about the Lord's servants during His absence. The first is that *believers possess God-given capacities*. The talents were given to each servant "according to his ability." By way of application, this corresponds to the natural talents possessed by virtue of creation (Ps. 139:13-16) and the spiritual gifts bestowed at regeneration. The abilities possessed by these servants undoubtedly involved different levels of fiscal, managerial, and vocational skill, all of which were to be used for their master.

Though it is not emphasized in this parable, the divine origin of all talents and gifts is a profound biblical truth. The believer recognizes that his body belongs to the Lord by virtue of redemption and indwelling (1 Cor. 6:19-20); that it is to be presented to God as a living sacrifice so that all of life becomes spiritual worship (Rom. 12:1); and that he is to love the Lord his God with all his heart, soul, mind, and strength (Mark 12:30). Since the body is the Lord's, all that we are is used to serve Him. We love Him when we employ His gifts to us "with strength."

There are often unnoticed dangers with excellent gifts. One is pride, a subtle desire to take credit for what we possess. But, as Paul asked the Corinthians, "Who makes you different from anyone else? What do you have that you did not receive? And if you did receive it, why do you boast as though you did not?" (1 Cor. 4:7, NIV) A second subtle danger is that our gifts can become the enemy of excellence of character. An obsession to develop particular abilities without a corresponding concern to develop one's character and fulfill one's responsibilities produces a misshapen life. We all carry memories of athletes, actors, or businessmen whose virtuoso performances were not accompanied by virtuous characters. The corrective is to realize that we are the Lord's servants. He determines not only which gifts we possess but also which gifts we are to develop and how we are to use them. Just as a need does not necessarily constitute God's call, our abilities do not necessarily determine our responsibilities. The Lord alone directs the believer's life.

A second message of the parable is that *believers possess God-given opportunities.* It is unfortunate that the meaning of the parable is obscured by the meaning of the English word *talents,* as well as by the decision of translators to transliterate the Greek term, *talanton,* rather than to find an appropriate translation. Confusing as it may seem, "talent" in the parable does not refer to an individual's talent or capability. This is evident from the fact that the master gave talents "to each according to his own ability." Thus ability was the reason for the gift, not the content of it. The entrustment of money (the talents) provided a means for these servants to use their talents (abilities). A "talent" in the Lord's parable thus represents an opportunity to use one's abilities for the Lord.

The parable, then, teaches that individuals possess not only diverse abilities, but also diverse opportunities. There is proportion between the two. The Lord gives opportunities on the basis of ability, since to have more than one could manage for the Lord would be a burden, not a blessing. Believers are equal neither in talents nor opportunities. However, the opportunities He does give are immense. Even the least able of the servants in Jesus' parable was entrusted with the equivalent of half a million dollars!

A third principle is that *believers possess God-given responsibilities.* The talents were not the servants' but their Lord's. We are accountable as stewards for the gifts God has given, and we are to use them for His purposes and His glory, not our own (cf. 1 Peter 4:10-11). Talents are given while the Master is absent in heaven, but they will be submitted to Him on His return, since responsibility means accountability. We are therefore stewards, not owners, of our gifts and opportunities. As D.L. Moody once observed, "Life is simply a stewardship and not an ownership, a trust and not a gift. With a gift you may do as you please, but with a trust you must give an account." Whether it is my talents, my time, my treasure, or the temple of my body, in all these I am only a steward.

THE APPROVAL OF THE MASTER

Two of the servants responded immediately and appropriately to their master's trust. They accepted the responsibility they were given and set out to invest their gifts. They were successful, not because of good fortune, but because of hard work (the word translated *traded* actually means "worked"). Because of diligent investment, each made a 100 percent gain—the first gaining an additional five talents, the other, two.

The Lord then describes the return of the master, after considerable delay, when he settles accounts with his servants. Each of the two successful servants appears before the master and receives virtually identical interviews. Both have a sense of pride and elation about their achievements: "Master, you entrusted five [two] talents to me; see, I have gained five [two] more talents." The master's response is equally enthusiastic: "Well done, good and faithful slave; you were faithful with a few things, I will put you in charge of many things; enter into the joy of your master." His exclamation is an expression of genuine joy and approval: "Excellent! Good work!" Obviously, he is delighted with their accomplishments.

The principles here taught by the Lord about the stewardship of talents are extremely important, since church-age believers also will settle accounts one day. At the Judgment Seat of Christ, every believer will "give account of himself to God" (Rom. 14:12) and will "be recompensed for his deeds in the body, according to what he has done, whether good or bad" (2 Cor. 5:10). The message of this parable is entirely consistent with what is taught elsewhere about that occasion.

The first principle the parable establishes is that excellent stewardship involves risk. It was precisely because the servants became vulnerable to failure and loss that they succeeded. God-given gifts and opportunities require both hard work and risk if they are to produce gain. There was no way for these men to "play it safe" *and* to be obedient.

Excellence also inevitably requires learning to withstand criticism. A friend named Richard Froude once wrote to Thomas Carlyle about the critics who seemed to be constantly attacking him:

The mists of criticism do hang about a mountain. Men who want no mists must be content with plains and deserts. Mists come with mountains. Soon the mists will evaporate, and the mountain will stand out in all its grandeur in the morning sunlight. Multitudes will stay in the valley, for there are few who aspire to reach the summit.[1]

There may be little consolation in recognizing that a commitment to excellence involves risk, but the reality is inescapable. Teddy Roosevelt put this element into proper perspective in a speech delivered at Paris' Sorbonne in 1910, two years after his presidency ended and two years before his abortive pursuit of a third term:

It is not the critic who counts; not the man who points out how the strong man stumbles, or where the doer of deeds could have done them better. The credit belongs to the man who is actually in the arena, whose face is marred by dust and sweat and blood; who strives valiantly; who errs, and comes short again and again; because there is not effort without error and shortcoming; but who does actually strive to do the deeds; who knows the great enthusiasms, the great devotions; who spends himself in a worthy cause, who at the best knows in the end the triumphs of high achievement and who at the worst, if he fails, at least fails while daring greatly, so that his place shall never be with those cold and timid souls who know neither victory nor defeat.[2]

The second principle taught is that reward is on the basis of responsibility, not capability. The two-talent man received exactly the same reward as the man of five talents. God's approval is proportional to capacity, not to quantity. Both servants received the commendation, "Excellent, well done!" though the amount they gained was greatly different. Excellence of performance is relative to ability; thus God honors His servants on the basis of the excellence of their work, not the sheer quantity of it. The excellence of a Volkswagen is not the excellence of a Ferrari, but both are excellent in their own way.

A third principle is that reward is disproportional to

service. As the Lord indicates, faithfulness with a little is rewarded by authority over much. Undoubtedly, the ultimate reference of the Lord's words is to the messianic kingdom, where believers will share in His glorious reign. The kingdom nature of the reward is further suggested by the parallel between "enter into the joy of your master" (vv. 21, 23) and the invitation to the sheep in verse 34, "Inherit the kingdom prepared for you from the foundation of the world." The Lord Jesus indicates that His rewards bear no relationship to human merit. It is a reward of grace. It is also a reward of increased responsibility and opportunity. The slave has become a ruler simply because he has been faithful to his responsibilities.

THE DISAPPROVAL OF THE MASTER

The third servant is a study in contrasts. While the immediate reaction of the others was to invest the money, his was to hide it. The burial of $500,000 was an act of considerable irresponsibility. At the least, he was a careless steward—anyone could have stumbled upon the treasure. Perhaps he was more than careless. While the motive for his action is not suggested, clearly the third servant had little faith in or regard for his master; in fact, he seems to have doubted that his master would return at all. In that case, the hidden money would be his to use as he pleased.

The story is told of a dying man who gave a large amount of cash to three friends, with a solemn charge that the money was to be placed with him in his casket. A few days after the funeral, his friends met. As they reminisced about their dead friend, one man suddenly blurted out his confession that he had put in most, but not all, of the money. Chagrined, a second man told a similar story. Righteously indignant, the third friend spoke his condemnation: "Gentlemen, I'm ashamed of you. I want you to know I put in my personal check for the whole amount." Perhaps our servant was of the latter variety!

For a considerable time, the money lay buried. Finally, the servant was summoned before his master and immediately launched into a self-justifying explanation. But his words are self-contradictory and self-condemning. He first reveals an attitude toward his lord which borders on contempt: "Master, I knew you to be a hard man, reaping where you did not sow, and gathering where you scattered no seed." The rest of the parable reveals that his accusation is patently false. The master has revealed himself, in his treatment of the other servants, to be a man of grace and generosity. But this servant is willfully ignorant of his master and therefore misrepresents his character.

The wicked servant lives in a world of excuses and irresponsibility. He claims that, because he feared failure, he had not risked investing the talent. Rather, he had buried it, then returned it with words almost deliberately contemptuous: "See, you have what is yours." The fact is, of course, that he had not avoided risk at all. By burying the money, he had exposed it to a multitude of dangers beyond his control. He was willing to risk the theft of the money, but not the investment of it. This also displays his contempt of the master. He had no desire to see the master's wealth increase and was therefore negligent with the master's trust.

The attitudes of this man deserve careful consideration. *First, he lacked knowledge of and respect for his master.* Our attitude toward the Lord will have a direct bearing on our attitude toward our God-given gifts and abilities. Neglect of our talents may reveal a lack of love to the One who gave them. *Second, he was afraid to take risks.* Douglas MacArthur's words about war surely apply to the subject of excellence: "Every mistake in war is excusable except inactivity and a refusal to take risks." *Third, he engaged in excuse-making.* Had he been nearly as diligent in investing his gifts as he was in devising excuses, the story would have been very different. As Benjamin Franklin observed: "The man who is good for excuses is good for little else." George Washington Carver concurred: "Ninety-nine percent of failures come from people who have the habit of making excuses." *Fourth, he was irresponsible.* He tried to avoid accepting a mature accountability for his actions.

The master's words to the servant are biting and direct. He is characterized for his wickedness, rebuked for his negligence, stripped of his responsibility, and condemned to the place of judgment. There is little doubt that the parable depicts the eternal judgment of this servant. The symbols of outer darkness, weeping, and gnashing of teeth are used elsewhere in Matthew's Gospel to describe the final destiny of unbelievers (8:12; 13:42; 24:51). Such an attitude toward the Lord and

His gifts is clear evidence of the absence of regeneration. This individual has not lost his salvation; he never possessed it. He is a servant only in the sense that all Jews can be said to possess that privileged position. The other parables in the Olivet Discourse also follow this pattern, as the Lord describes evil servants (24:48-51) and foolish virgins (25:1-13).

A fundamental principle is contained in the master's words to his other servants: "For to everyone who has shall more be given, and he shall have an abundance; but from the one who does not have, even what he does have shall be taken away" (v. 29). Opportunities given by God and neglected are lost and further opportunity is denied. On the other hand, faithful service is rewarded by enlarged opportunity. Negligence is punished and diligence is honored. The wicked servant's neglect of his responsibility revealed his lack of faith and rendered his actions irremediable. While a believer cannot lose his salvation, he can waste his opportunities. The Judgment Seat will be a time of reward on the basis of "what he has done, whether good or bad." Paul uses a word conveying the idea of that which is "worthless," rather than that which is morally bad. The false servant did not commit an immoral act, but his actions were worthless, since they made no contribution to the master's cause. In the same way, our works may be wood, hay, or stubble (1 Cor. 3:12, KJV). They have no lasting value, and in the Day of Christ will be unalterably consumed, so that the believer is left empty-handed before his Lord.

The question may be asked as to why it was the one-talent servant who failed. The only satisfactory answer is that it is an arbitrary detail of the parable. It could equally well have been the five-talent man. As Parker aptly comments:

> The ground which received the one talent will also receive the five; you can easily find a spade to dig a grave for your talents and abilities, your money and your time, but understand that in burying your talent you are burying yourself; in burying anything that God has given you, you are burying part of your very life.[3]

THE EXPRESSION OF EXCELLENCE

The Parable of the Talents puts the issue of gifts and abilities into a very helpful context. God has endowed every individual with natural abilities and every believer with spiritual gifts. Also, in accordance with His individual purpose for every believer and His knowledge of each person, He assigns opportunities to exercise those gifts. Just as our gifts differ, so do our opportunities and responsibilities. Every range of talent and sphere of opportunity is a means to serve the Lord, to invest gifts for His purposes and not merely our own. There is no rupture of life into "the sacred" and "the secular." All of life is God's, and therefore all of life is an arena for true excellence.

Excellence is the maximum exercise of one's gifts and abilities within the range of responsibilities given by God. The last point is very important. Because it is God who determines excellence, it is unique for every individual. For example, a pianist who knows himself called by God to be a concert musician, and a pianist who is also a husband, elder, and businessman may possess exactly the same level of musical potential. But God holds one responsible for a different level of performance than the other simply because He has called each to a distinct mix of responsibilities and opportunities. A seven-year-old pianist obviously measures excellence in an entirely different way than a professional musician. But whatever the apparent excellence of one as compared to the other, God gives to each, as he is faithful, the same word of approval: "Excellent." After all, the five-talent man was by all appearances "better" than the two-talent man. But eternity revealed different criteria.

The concept of excellence is therefore inseparable from the doctrine of the lordship of Christ. God has vested in each individual expressions of His creativity. There is rich variety both in the nature of His gifts and their quality. But the gifts He bestows are not autonomous. They are to be exercised in conformity to His moral will and in harmony with His individual guidance of the believer. The Parable of the Talents indicates that the exercise of gifts and abilities is to be in submission to the Lord who gave them. Our gifts are for His use. They must not be buried when He calls us to employ them. But when He does not encourage the use of all the gifts He has graciously bestowed, we can be confident that He has other opportunities for us to pursue.

CHAPTER SEVEN

THE POSTURE OF EXCELLENCE

By his mid-thirties, Winston Churchill was by far the most successful politician of his age in Britain. His career had been like a brilliant meteor blazing across the sky. The son of a notorious politician, he had achieved fame as a reporter and author whose chief subject matter was his own military adventures. Elected to Parliament at the tender age of twenty-five, he entered the Cabinet at thirty-one, and at the outbreak of World War I, was Lord of the Admiralty and part of the War Cabinet. Intelligent, hardworking, eloquent, single-minded, ambitious—the world lay at his feet. But Churchill's world revolved around him as the sun. He was more interested in himself and his own ideas than in anything else and his peers were reluctant to trust him.

Then, in 1915, his world collapsed. A military expedition at Gallipoli for which he was held responsible (critics still debate the validity of the charge) turned into a bloody debacle. He was forced to resign from the Cabinet and his long years in the political wilderness, with intermittent respites, began. One biography gives this period of his life the fascinating title, "The Rise to Failure."

In the crucible of failure, Churchill forged some new qualities which became instrumental in his success as the great Allied leader during World War II. But until he refocused his life, he was a brilliant failure. *Achievement in itself can never be the mark of excellence or greatness.*

The concepts of excellence and greatness are closely allied. Though greatness may be defined in a multitude of ways from the human perspective, almost invariably it describes the superior exercise of human talents or outstanding feats of personal achievement. To say that Winston Churchill was a great political leader differs very little from saying that he displayed excellence in leadership. To ascribe greatness to a book is to affirm that the author achieved a measure of excellence in his work. The two terms are not synonyms, but they do move in the same realm. To speak of excellence is to speak of what has supreme value and also to ascribe to it some form of greatness.

The Bible insists that true greatness cannot be known from a purely human viewpoint. From the grandiose claims of the citizens of Babel to the satanic self-deification of the Antichrist, the sweep of human history demonstrates the emptiness and futility of all man-centered claims to greatness. The apparent greatness of human achievements and performances appears absurd when measured by the One who alone is great. True excellence, true greatness, can be evaluated only in light of the incarnation and instruction of the Lord Jesus.

The Lord Jesus addresses the subject of true greatness most explicitly in the incident recorded in Matthew 20:20-28. However, the message contained there is one often on His lips in His instructions to His disciples. Far more significantly, it is a central theme of His entire life and ministry. By affirming that the only true greatness is to be found in servanthood, the Lord Jesus not only turns the world's values upside down, He totally redirects the concept of excellence. The notion that excellence involves servanthood would be utterly inconceivable to Homer, Aristotle, or Nietzsche. But the posture of the servant, taught by the Lord Jesus in Matthew 20 and modeled by Him throughout His life, is, for the Christian, the posture of excellence. This is a theme essential to the Christian concept of excellence since it is a direct repudiation of excellence as elitism, the prerogative of the uniquely gifted.

It must be noted that, by stressing servanthood, the Lord places an emphasis on what a believer is rather than on what he does. Servanthood involves actions, but it flows from attitudes. A servant, therefore, is an individual with a revolutionary attitude toward himself and toward others because of his relationship to the Lord.

John 13:1-16 is the supreme illustration of the excellence of servanthood as the Lord washes His disciples' feet, while Matthew 20:20-28 is the central exposition of the concept. The Matthew passage thus provides a useful framework for considering the relationship of excellence to servanthood:

> Then the mother of the sons of Zebedee came to Him with her sons, bowing down, and making a request of Him. And He said to her, "What do you wish?" She said to Him, "Command that in Your kingdom these two sons of mine may sit one on Your right and one on Your left." But Jesus answered and said, "You do not know what you are asking for. Are you able to drink the cup that I am about to drink?" They said to Him, "We are able." He said to them, "My cup you shall drink; but to sit on My right and on My left, this is not Mine to give, but it is for those for whom it has been prepared by My Father." And hearing this, the ten became indignant at the two brothers.
> But Jesus called them to Himself, and said, "You know that the rulers of the Gentiles lord it over them, and their great men exercise authority over them. It is not so among you, but whoever wishes to become great among you shall be your servant, and whoever wishes to be first among you shall be your slave; just as the Son of man did not come to be served, but to serve, and to give His life a ransom for many."

The Gospels reveal that the disciples were fascinated by the subject of greatness. More than once the question surfaced; occasionally it even produced open dispute among the disciples (cf. Matt. 18:1ff; Luke 14:7ff; 22:24-30). An open argument among grown men about who is greatest strikes the modern reader as rather bizarre. The fact is that we have found less obvious ways to carry on the debate. Status symbols, official titles, and carefully cultivated images are merely contemporary ways to make the same point in more subtle ways. However, in Jewish society the question was inescapable, as it is in any hierarchical society. Society was stratified by economic status, social class, religious persuasion, and age categories, and these distinctions were never irrelevant. As Schlatter observes:

At all points, in worship, in the administration of justice, at meals, in all dealings, there constantly arose the question of who was the greater and estimating the honor due to each was a task which had constantly to be filled and was felt to be very important.[1]

Thus the issues raised in this account were of immense practical importance to the disciples, and the Lord's answer must have seemed incredibly radical.

THE PROBLEM OF GREATNESS

It is difficult to imagine a more inappropriate time for a request motivated by selfish ambition than this incident records. The Lord Jesus had only recently concluded His third prediction of His forthcoming death and resurrection (Matt. 20:17-19). Apparently oblivious to the real meaning of the Lord's prediction, the disciples petition Jesus for a position of personal greatness. Nor is this the only such demonstration of spiritual obtuseness. An earlier prediction by the Lord of His death (Matt. 17:22-23) was closely followed by a question from the disciples about greatness (Matt. 18:1). And the Lord's last Passover meal with His men, an event of immense significance to Him, is also marred by a childish dispute about greatness (Luke 22:24-30). The dramatic contrast between the Lord's acute suffering and the disciples' total insensitivity demonstrates the dramatically different value systems they represent. The concept of excellence as servanthood taught by the Lord is totally foreign to the mindset of the natural man.

According to Matthew, it was the mother of James and John who approached Jesus. A comparison of Matthew 27:56, Mark 15:40, and John 19:25 strongly suggests that their mother was Salome, the sister of the Lord's mother, Mary. Mark, however, attributes the question to the boys themselves (Mark 10:35), and in Matthew the Lord's answer is addressed not to Salome but to her sons. This all suggests that the two men were using their mother as the spokesperson for their ambitions, perhaps believing that a request from Aunt Salome would carry more weight with the Lord.

The request of Zebedee's wife demonstrates great faith and respect. Her humble posture and respectful request are evidence of a deep conviction that Jesus is the Messiah. Indeed, the very premise of her question is that He will come in His kingdom, with the authority to grant positions of power. She knows that He will be on the central throne in the kingdom, and her request is based on His promise that each of the twelve disciples would likewise occupy a throne in that time of glory (Matt. 19:28). Salome's request is thus a remarkable demonstration of personal faith in Christ.

However, her request also reveals selfishness. "Grant that these two sons of mine may sit, one on your right and one on your left" is a request that James and John be made the chief ministers of the Lord. Such positions would be ones of prestige, power, and privilege. We all respond to such things. But her eyes were so filled with future glory for her sons that she totally ignored the Lord's words about betrayal, beating, and crucifixion (Matt. 20:18). Did she really desire her sons to be on the right or left of someone hanging on a cross? But apart from the Cross, there could be no kingdom.

The Lord Jesus answers her request with a stinging rebuke: "You do not know what you are asking for" (Matt. 20:22). The law of the kingdom is that those who suffer with Him are those who will live and reign with Him (2 Tim. 2:11-12). To enjoy the kingdom means enduring the Cross. Therefore, the Lord asks them, "Are you able to drink the cup which I am about to drink?" (Matt. 20:22) The cup is an Old Testament metaphor of God's wrath and His judgment on sins (Ps. 75:8; Isa. 51:17; Jer. 25:15ff; 49:12), and this is undoubtedly what the Lord Jesus has in mind as He anticipates the Cross. To drink His cup is to share His fate.

James and John reply with a brash, "We are able (Matt. 20:22). They have little idea of what they are saying, but are absolutely certain that they possess the attributes necessary for spiritual authority. They are able to drink Christ's cup and are worthy to share in His reign. Their self-confidence is supreme.

The Lord does not warn them against presumption. Instead, He simply affirms that they will indeed drink His cup. This can only mean that they will share His fate of suffering, rejection, and even death, a prediction fulfilled in James' death as the first apostolic martyr and John's long experience of suffering and imprisonment for His Lord. But places of privilege in the kingdom are the prerogative of the Father. He first prepares the man for a position, then prepares the position for the man. These disciples will drink the cup of suffering before they will know the prepared throne of blessing. Thus suffering, service, and responsibility are all preparation for privilege in the kingdom. Authority is not immediately granted to those who are the first to ask, but to those who are divinely approved. In the following verses, this concept is emphasized. Where we sit (our greatness) in the kingdom will depend on whether we serve in the family of believers.

A mother whale once warned her son, "Remember, it's when you go to the top and start blowing that you get harpooned." The brothers' presumptuous request certainly aroused the anger of the other disciples. One suspects, however, that they were not nearly as upset at the content of the brothers' request as they were that someone else would get there first. They resented the devious method of Zebedee's sons, but they themselves were no more sensitive to the Lord's heart. For them also, greatness involved power and position, and therefore they too stood in need of a revolutionary change in values.

THE PRINCIPLE OF TRUE GREATNESS

The ways of the world have changed little in twenty centuries and the Lord's words portray an immense contrast between the way of the world and the way of the disciple. Gentile greatness takes many forms. We surround our leaders with special privileges and honors which elevate them above others. Security systems shut them off from the ordinary world and a host of people stand ready to cater to their every need or whim. Even in a society proud of its democratic political system, we promote our politicians, superstars, and rock idols to pedestals from which they exercise their power. The cult of personalities and celebrities has a host of worshipers and our fascination with the favored elite is shown by the magazines and television programs devoted to such subjects.

The disciples knew well the Gentile pattern of leadership. They lived their lives under the heavy hand of Rome, suffering the countless indignities which were forced on them as a subservient people. Caesar's distant power was a very present reality in their daily lives through the structure of Roman political and military figures. But the same pattern existed within Gentile society. Though Roman citizens had rights unknown to the Jews, their rulers and great ones operated on the principles of domination and power-wielding. "Lord it over" emphasizes the oppression of Gentile rule, and in 1 Peter 5:3, the verb expresses a domineering attitude which exploits people rather than serves them. "Exercise authority" describes the authoritarianism and officiousness of Gentile greatness by which a position becomes a weapon to use on others rather than a tool to serve them. The Lord's description recorded in Luke 22:25 is similar in emphasis: "The kings of the Gentiles lord it over them; and those who are in authority over them are called 'Benefactors.' " Such titles were even more familiar in the ancient world than today. Octavius was "the August one—Caesar Augustus," and honorifics such as Excellency, Benefactor, and "He who deserves adoration" were commonplace. The point of all these titles was to create distance and prestige. The great were praised, served, and feared, for theirs were positions of power. The secular principle is clear. The great rule and the great are served.

A fascinating contemporary illustration of the Gentile attitude toward leadership is found in Richard Nixon's *Leaders*. Two quotations will suffice:

> No one becomes a major leader without a strong will, or without a strong ego. Lately it has become fashionable to try to conceal ego, to pretend that it does not exist, to present instead an outward modesty. But I have never known a major leader who was not an egotist. Some of these leaders affected a modest air, but none was a modest person. Modesty was a pose, a device, just as MacArthur's corncob pipe was a device and Churchill's strut was a pose. A person has to believe in himself if he is to win mastery over the forces leaders have to deal with. He has to believe in his cause if he is going to punish himself the way leaders must. Unless he believes in himself, he is not going to persuade others to believe in him.[2]
>
> By the same token, the "great" leader is not necessarily good. Adolf Hitler electrified a nation. Joseph Stalin was brutally effective at wielding power. Ho Chi Minh became a folk hero to millions beyond the borders of Vietnam. The good and the bad alike can be equally driven, equally determined, equally skilled, equally persuasive.

Leadership itself is morally neutral; it can be used for good or for ill.

Thus, virtue is not what lifts great leaders above others. Others are more virtuous but less successful. The maxim, "Nice guys finish last," is far more applicable to politics than to sports. What lifts great leaders above the second-raters is that they are more forceful, more resourceful, and have a shrewdness of judgment that spares them the fatal error and enables them to identify the fleeting opportunity.[3]

Such assumptions, natural and necessary as they are made to appear, have no place in the fellowship of believers. The Lord's words are clear and unmistakable: "It is not so among you" (Matt. 20:26). He has set in motion an entirely new pattern which does not abolish the concept of greatness, but totally redefines it for His people. In so doing, He revolutionizes the concept of excellence. Authority is replaced with ministry. Power is transformed into service. The ambition to sit on a throne in splendor gives way to a willingness to wait on tables in humility.

The term the Lord Jesus uses to describe the believer as a servant is the Greek word *diakonos*, familiar in our word *deacon*. The word itself describes menial and mundane activities, such as waiting on tables or caring for household needs. A servant was necessarily dependent on others, his time and freedom severely limited, and his actions defined by those in authority over him. Such a life the Greeks viewed as degrading and dishonorable. The thought that one would voluntarily choose servitude was unimaginable. As Hess observes, "In general, voluntary giving of oneself in service of one's fellow man is alien to Greek thought. The highest goal before a man was the development of his own personality."[4] Beyer gives a helpful summary of the Greek attitude:

In Greek eyes, servmg is not very dignified. Ruling and not serving is proper to a man. . . . The formula of the sophist: "How can a man be happy when he has to serve someone?" expresses the basic Greek attitude. . . . Service acquires a higher value only when it is rendered to the state. . . . For the Greek in his wisdom and freedom there can certainly be no question of his existing to serve others.[5]

The attitude toward service within Judaism was not dissimilar to that of the Greeks. Though service was held to be a responsibility for a pious Jew, in practice it was done largely as an act of social obligation or as a duty to those of higher rank. When servitude was practiced, it bore little resemblance to the pattern of life described by the Lord Jesus. Hess captures the Jewish attitude:

> Though Judaism in the time of Jesus knew and practiced its social responsibilities, e.g., to the poor, this was done mainly by alms, not by serving (cf. Luke 10:30-35). Lowly service, e.g., waiting at table, was beneath the dignity of a free man (cf. Luke 7:44ff). Sometimes, the greater would wait at table, but this was unusual.[6]

It is important to recognize that there was nothing in either Jewish or Greek society which corresponded with the Lord's teaching. It was radical and unprecedented.

The first principle of servanthood is therefore that kingdom living is not based on the law of the world, but on the law of love. "It shall not be so among you" emphasizes that, in the fellowship of believers, the Lord Jesus is the model, not the great ones of earth. The law of entrance into the kingdom is childlike humility (Matt. 18:1-5), and the law of life in the kingdom is Christlike service to others. There is no spiritual aristocracy who have elite privileges. To be a slave or a servant is contemptible in the world's eyes, but it is a mark of excellence in the believer. Both the pattern and prerogatives of the kingdom are radically different from the world's value structure.

A second principle is that servanthood is self-chosen, not imposed. "Whoever wishes to be great . . ." indicates the voluntary nature of servanthood. A slave served under compulsion of force; a Christian is to serve under the compulsion of love. The believer has an obligation of obedience fed by a motivation of gratitude. The Lord reinforces this voluntary nature of service when He teaches His disciples: "Let him who is the greatest among you become as the youngest, and the leader as the servant. For who is greater, the one who reclines at the table, or the one who serves? Is it not the one who reclines at the table? But I am among you as the One who serves" (Luke 22:26-27). The Lord Jesus certainly chose to serve and overcame Peter's opposition to His choice (John 13:6-10). In the same way, believers are to desire the place of servanthood. In a society where youngers served their elders and where followers waited on leaders, disciples were to choose what no one could expect or demand.

The nature of servanthood deserves careful consideration. A servant is one who has accepted a responsibility for another and therefore has given up certain personal freedoms. His movements are restricted by others. He is willing to bear the weight of responsibility which others would rather avoid. Abraham Lincoln beautifully modeled this attitude. After the Battle of Gettysburg, General Lee's Confederate forces were vulnerable to attack from the rear as they retreated to Virginia. Lincoln was sensitive to the fact that General Meade was new to the command of the Army of the Potomac and was feeling new burdens of leadership. Therefore he sent sealed orders to attack, enclosing a personal note to Meade: "The order I enclose is not on record. If you succeed you need not publish it. Then, if you succeed, you will have all the credit of the movement. If not, I'll take the responsibility." Such is the attitude of a servant.

A servant is also one who is willing to meet needs and to pay the price of meeting needs. When feet are dirty, a servant washes them (John 13:1-20). When a table requires a waiter, a servant waits on tables (Luke 22:27). As Hess comments, "When we speak of serving, we imply work done for another, either voluntarily or compulsorily, the benefit of which will accrue to the one for whom it has been done."[7] A servant is also willing to forego praise. He does not act to be honored or applauded, but simply out of love toward his brothers. This is a characteristic of servanthood the Lord Jesus spells out in graphic detail. Having just described the Pharisees with their love of praise, prominence, and prestige, He describes how a disciple is to live (Matt. 23:8-12):

But do not be called Rabbi; for One is your Teacher, and you are all brothers. And do not call anyone on earth

your father; for One is your Father, He who is in heaven.
And do not be called leaders; for One is your Leader, that
is, Christ. But the greatest among you shall be your servant. And whoever exalts himself shall be humbled; and
whoever humbles himself shall be exalted.

The late Indira Gandhi once stated, "My grandfather
once told me that there are two kinds of people—those who
take the work and those who take the credit. He told me to try
to be in the first group for there is much less competition
there." Whether Mrs. Gandhi lived up to her grandfather's
advice is debatable, but the perspective is that of a servant.
The servant of the Lord may not care which other people get
the credit, but he cares greatly that his Lord gets the credit.

A large group of European pastors came to one of D.L.
Moody's Northfield Bible Conferences in Massachusetts in the
late 1800s. Following the European custom of the time, each
guest put his shoes outside his room to be cleaned by the hall
servants overnight. But of course this was America and there
were no hall servants.

Walking the dormitory halls that night, Moody saw the
shoes and determined not to embarrass his brothers. He mentioned the need to some ministerial students who were there,
but met with only silence or pious excuses. Moody returned to
the dorm, gathered up the shoes, and, alone in his room, the
world's most famous evangelist began to clean and polish the
shoes. Only the unexpected arrival of a friend in the midst of
the work revealed the secret.

When the foreign visitors opened their doors the next
morning, their shoes were shined. They never knew by
whom. Moody told no one, but his friend told a few people,
and during the rest of the conference, different men volun-
teered to shine the shoes in secret. Perhaps the episode is a
vital insight into why God used D.L. Moody as He did. He
was a man with a servant's heart and that was the basis of his
true greatness.

A third principle taught by the Lord Jesus is the nobility
of servanthood. Service is not a prerequisite for greatness or a
means to it. As Manson suggests, "In the kingdom of God,
service is not a stepping-stone to nobility; it *is* nobility, the
only kind of nobility that is recognized."[8] Faithful service, free-

ly chosen, in obedience to Christ, in a lowly place, is itself true greatness. Authority in the church should not come from prestige but from service, a principle almost totally ignored throughout church history. However, Paul states clearly that servanthood is the basis of authority (1 Cor. 16:15-16):

> Now I urge you, brethren (you know the household of Stephanas, that they were the first fruits of Achaia, and that they have devoted themselves for ministry to the saints), that you also be in subjection to such men, and to everyone who helps in the work and labors.

It is the servant ministry of such men that makes them the type of men to whom submission should be granted.

Though the Lord Jesus does not emphasize it in this context, it is important to recognize that the disciple of whom He speaks is not primarily a servant of men, but of Christ Himself. "If any one serves Me, let him follow Me; and where I am, there shall My servant also be" (John 12:26). The mark of a servant is imitation of the Lord Jesus. While he serves others, it is preeminently as a servant of the Saviour. As Torrance indicates:

> The servant is one who has been given a task by his Master, and who does only what is commanded by Him, and not what he thinks out for himself. . . . It is a form of service in which he is not partially but completely committed in the whole of his being before God, which he discharges not occasionally but continuously in the whole of his existence as a follower of Jesus Christ.[9]

THE PATTERN OF TRUE GREATNESS

As in every area of life, the Lord Jesus is the model for believers. The phrase "just as" which begins Matthew 20:28 indicates that His life is a precise model for the believer. We are to live "just as" He did, not in His spiritual accomplishments but in His personal principles. In the same way, when the Lord Jesus washes the feet of His disciples, He describes it as an example for His people (John 13:15). His practice becomes our pattern.

Matthew 20:28 is one of the great New Testament statements on the doctrine of salvation since in it the Lord clearly affirms His self-understanding of the Cross as an act of substitutionary atonement. He died in our place. However, His primary purpose is to describe His life as a servant and to emphasize the total reversal He represents of all human ideas of greatness and rank. His life embodies infinite authority, infinite humility, and infinite ministry. His infinite authority is indicated by the messianic title "Son of man" (cf. Dan. 7:1-14) and the recognition that He is the preexistent Lord of glory. His infinite humility is revealed in the statement of His incarnation and condescension. He came, not to be served, but to serve. All that He became as a man, meek and lowly, born in poverty, living in humility and serving as a footwasher to His disciples, is alluded to in that pregnant expression. But the depth of His servanthood is demonstrated by His ultimate ministry of self-sacrifice. He gave His life a ransom for many.

The Lord Jesus lived all His life as a servant. He served men by *doing the will of God*, living all His life under the directions of His Father. He also served men by *teaching the Word of God*, setting before them the truths of His Father. Above all, He served men by *displaying the love of God*, in life and, supremely, in death. In all these ways, the Lord displayed His greatness and eternal excellence. Thus, in one succinct sentence, the Lord Jesus not only summarized His own life, but encapsulated Christian life and ministry.

It is thus apparent that a discussion of biblical excellence is incomplete without a consideration of servanthood. It was a central theme of the Lord's model of excellence and it is a central theme of His teaching about a believer's lifestyle.

Almost inevitably, discussions of excellence are related to considerations of success. Excellence of performance is seen as the means to recognition or material reward. The Lord provides an important counterweight to such ideas. Excellence of performance alone cannot be true greatness. In God's eyes only the servant is great. There is thus a significant danger in excellence. The very honors we bestow on perceived excellence may hinder its development in an individual; if he begins to place value on the privileges of excellence, he is in danger of ignoring what the Lord teaches about the pathway to it. It is certainly not wrong to praise outstanding performances. But such praise often produces prima donnas rather than servants.

THE POSTURE OF EXCELLENCE

Unless we recognize that God's pathway to true excellence and greatness is entirely different than the world's, we will misunderstand the nature of excellence, we will misdirect our energies toward excellence, and we will mistake the demonstration of excellence. True excellence always takes the posture of a servant.

CHAPTER EIGHT

THE COST OF EXCELLENCE

Bertoldo de Giovanni is a name even the most enthusiastic lover of art is unlikely to recognize. In his time, he was an important sculptor but none of his work has lasted. His chief claim to fame is as a historical connector. He was the pupil of Donatello, the greatest sculptor of his time, and the teacher of Michelangelo, the greatest sculptor of all time.

Michelangelo was only fourteen years old when he came to Bertoldo, but it was already obvious that he was enormously gifted. Bertoldo was wise enough to realize that gifted people are often tempted to coast rather than to grow, and therefore he kept trying to pressure his young prodigy to work seriously at his art. One day, he came into the studio to find Michelangelo toying with a piece of sculpture far beneath his abilities. Bertoldo grabbed a hammer, stomped across the room, and smashed the work into tiny pieces, shouting his unforgettable message: "Michelangelo, talent is cheap; dedication is costly!"

What separates people is not so much their innate abilities as their motivation. Few of us live up to our potential. Professional coaches point out that the difference between the star and the superstar is usually not talent, but motivation: one is willing to pay a price that the other isn't. The same factor applies in most areas of life. Excellence does not always require great gifts so much as great commitment. As Gardner perceptively writes:

THE COST OF EXCELLENCE

Some people may have greatness thrust upon them. Very few have excellence thrust upon them. They achieve it. They do not achieve it unwittingly, by "doin' what comes naturally"; and they don't stumble into it in the course of amusing themselves. All excellence involves discipline and tenacity of purpose.[1]

Only a person possessed by an ingrained dissatisfaction with the status quo and the mediocre will be activated to set high goals and to pay the price of reaching them. Excellence of achievement requires the single-minded development of talents and abilities, rejecting the belief that good is good enough.

No one demonstrates more clearly the tenacious pursuit of excellence than the Apostle Paul. He was a man undoubtedly possessed of unusual gifts, both natural and spiritual. But Paul's secret was to be found not in his abilities, but in his heart. In his first letter to the church at Corinth, he describes his intense determination to fulfill God's purpose for his life (1 Cor. 9:24-27):

Do you know that those who run in a race all run, but only one receives the prize? Run in such a way that you may win. And everyone who competes in the games exercises self-control in all things. They then do it to receive a perishable wreath, but we an imperishable. Therefore I run in such a way, as not without aim; I box in such a way, as not beating the air; but I buffet my body and make it my slave, lest possibly, after I have preached to others, I myself should be disqualified.

However, the most extensive statement of Paul's pursuit of excellence and the price he paid in the process is found in the Epistle to the Philippians. If Paul achieved an unusual level of excellence, it was because he paid an unusual price for excellence. Yet that price is required of all who seek to realize God's purpose of excellence.

Only an understanding of what Paul was as an unbeliever can clarify what it cost him to become what he did. He had experienced a revolutionary change of values which entirely redirected his life. But excellence is not achieved by a price paid once. There was a continuing cost for Paul which shaped his daily goals and values. In his life, superior talent was wedded to superior character and high motivation, and he eloquently describes the costs paid in the pursuit of excellence (Phil. 3:7-16):

> But whatever things were gain to me, those things I have counted as loss for the sake of Christ. More than that, I count all things to be loss in view of the surpassing value of knowing Christ Jesus my Lord, for whom I have suffered the loss of all things, and count them but rubbish in order that I may gain Christ, and may be found in Him, not having a righteousness of my own derived from the Law, but that which is through faith in Christ, the righteousness which comes from God on the basis of faith, that I may know Him, and the power of His resurrection and the fellowship of His sufferings, being conformed to His death; in order that I may attain to the resurrection from the dead.
>
> Not that I have already obtained it, or have already become perfect, but I press on in order that I may lay hold of that for which also I was laid hold of by Christ Jesus. Brethren, I do not regard myself as having laid hold of it yet; but one thing I do: forgetting what lies behind and reaching forward to what lies ahead, I press on toward the goal for the prize of the upward call of God in Christ Jesus.
>
> Let us therefore, as many as are perfect, have this attitude; and if in anything you have a different attitude, God will reveal that also to you; however, let us keep living by that same standard to which we have attained.

The English novelist, J.B. Priestly, was once asked why several gifted writers with whom he had been associated in earlier years had not progressed in their work as he had. His answer was direct and simple: "Gentlemen, the difference between us was not in ability, but in the fact that they merely toyed with the fascinating idea of writing. I cared like blazes! It is this caring like the blazes that counts." Priestly is right that caring is what counts. But caring alone is not enough. It is important to care about the right things, about worthy values.

Paul was always a man who cared deeply, but spiritual excellence involved for him a revolutionary change of values.

THE COST OF CHANGED VALUES

As a proud Hebrew, Saul the Pharisee had been the epitome of Judaism. His credentials were impeccable and assured him of a position of prestige and power in the religious community of Palestine. In his attack on the carnal pretensions of the Judaizers, Paul enumerated his former values. By inheritance, he possessed certain advantages: "circumcised the eighth day, of the nation of Israel, of the tribe of Benjamin, a Hebrew of the Hebrews" (Phil. 3:5). All those were qualifications which placed him in the truest strain of Judaism. A strict Hebrew of the purest blood, he was deeply proud of his heritage. He was also proud of his acquired achievements: "as to the Law, a Pharisee; as to zeal, a persecutor of the church; as to the righteousness which is in the Law, found blameless" (Phil. 3:5-6). Belonging to the most orthodox loyalists of the Law, he was devoured by a zeal for Judaism which took the form of blind hatred against the followers of Christ. His obedience to the external requirements of the Law was rigorous and thorough.

The hold of those values on Paul was immensely powerful. They represented his basis for confidence before God and men. He was certain that such credentials assured him of divine approval and human esteem. But, in a moment, on the Damascus road, his values underwent a revolutionary change. Suddenly, having met the living Christ, he came to realize that everything he considered valuable was worthless, even detrimental. He had thought that God's approval came on the top rung of the ladder of achievement. Now he suddenly realized that his ladder was leaning on the wrong wall. His proud acts of self-righteousness could only produce a self-sufficiency which made salvation impossible; they could do nothing to remove his guilt before a holy God.

Paul's revolutionary new perspective called for a total reevaluation of his old credentials. He saw them as *loss*, a word used in Acts 27:10, 21 to describe valuable cargo which was jettisoned to save life. The picture is graphic. Such things have a certain value, but become a liability when salvation is in view. They are therefore disposable. The supposed assets of his former life he now saw as liabilities since they kept him from faith in the righteousness of Christ. Therefore, he forfeited them. He also saw these past credentials as *rubbish*, a very strong word which described refuse or human excrement. He felt actual contempt for all religious self-righteousness which excluded Jesus Christ. He would rather have nothing with Christ than all these things without Him. As Motyer incisively observes:

> Who would want to spend his life on a refuse heap? Far from regretting that they are gone or hankering to have them back, Paul no more wants them around than he wants a bad smell, if this is the appointed road to more and more of Christ. It is Christ, not "things," who satisfies.[2]

There is always a cost in a radical change of values. It dramatically alters one's relationships and perspectives. But for Paul, cost was swallowed up in privilege. He had not so much abandoned his old values as exchanged them for "the surpassing value of knowing Christ Jesus [his] Lord" (Phil. 3:8).

The choice of values is extremely important to the realization of excellence. As Peters and Waterman observe in their study of excellence, "So much of excellence in performance has to do with people's being motivated by compelling, simple—even beautiful—values."[3] After his conversion, Paul never doubted that ultimate value lay in "the surpassing value of knowing Christ Jesus my Lord." The word *surpassing* is a word of excellence, used by Paul in Philippians 4:7 to describe the peace of God "which surpasses all comprehension." It was used by the Greeks to describe the athlete in training who was pursuing victory in the games. Paul had no doubt about the gold medal of life. Life's supreme value was knowing Christ.

Paul's values, therefore, focused on the person of the Saviour. The supreme transaction of his life had occurred when he exchanged his old values for the knowledge of Christ, which brought salvation (Phil. 3:8). The supreme fact of his life was union with Christ, which was intimately linked with justification (v. 9). The supreme desire of his life was fellowship with Christ in knowledge and ministry (v. 10). Everything meaningful to Paul, in life or in death, was therefore related to the person of the Saviour. Whether fellowship with

Him involved resurrection power, painful suffering, or eternal glory, he was willing to pay the price. He knew all that mattered was intimate fellowship with his Lord.

The excellence of Paul's life is inseparable from the clarity of his goal, the excellence of the object of his goal, and the single-mindedness with which he pursued his goal. He had made an unequivocal choice of values and everything in life was subordinate to them. It should be observed that Paul is not only an example in the fact of his choice, but a model in the content of his choice. The spiritual facts which led Paul to speak of "the surpassing value of knowing Christ" are universals, which mean that no other choice is worthy from any person. The knowledge of Christ is the root of all true excellence.

THE COST OF CONCENTRATION

Paul's spiritual position in Christ, as described in Philippians 3:7-10, was perfect and complete. Nothing could be added to the perfect righteousness which he had found through faith in his Lord. But Paul was also aware that imputed righteousness was intended to produce practical righteousness in the believer. Therefore, in Philippians 3:12-16, he focuses on his spiritual condition. His position through faith was past perfect; his condition in life was imperfect progressive; his destiny in Christ is future perfect. Every believer lives in this "already, but not yet" tension, and Paul models the spiritual believer's response to it.

HIS COMPELLING PASSION. Paul lived under the conviction that God had a purpose for his life. Though he does not use the term, it is clearly implied in the phrase "that I may lay hold of that for which also I was laid hold of by Christ Jesus." The Lord Jesus had taken hold of his life for a purpose. Concerning Paul's person, Christ had a goal of Christlikeness. Concerning his ministry, the risen Lord had indicated the unique role he intended Paul to fulfill. Though Paul was laid hold of by the Lord in a unique way and for a unique ministry, there is nothing unique about the fact that God had a purpose for his life. For every believer, God has such a purpose.

Confident of God's purpose, Paul was compelled to achieve it. He was acutely aware of his present imperfection. "Not that I have already obtained it, or have already become perfect. . . . Brethren, I do not regard myself as having laid hold of it yet" (Phil. 3:12-13). Undoubtedly, this surprised many who were convinced that Paul "had it made." But his denial of perfection is stated in the most emphatic terms possible. It is also noteworthy that Paul does not compare himself with others. The only valid standards of evaluation are the purpose of God for one's life *and* the person of Christ. Both, Paul realizes, are far beyond him. He is a man in process, called to Christlikeness, and aware of his shortcomings.

However, his recognition of imperfection arouses desire, not discouragement. His attitude is that of a hunter relentlessly pursuing his prey—"I press on" (Phil. 3:12, 14). He is tenacious in his ambition; nothing here suggests a passivity which functions by the cliché, "Let go and let God." Spiritual excellence requires confident faith, but it also requires concerted effort.

HIS FOCUSED PURPOSE. Every individual is multifaceted and multitalented. Only a person who focuses his energies and unites his interests can achieve excellence. Paul was a man committed to "this one thing." He refused to be distracted or deflected from the one best thing God called him to do by the many good things he could do. It was D.L. Moody who observed, "I'd rather have a man who says 'This one thing I do' than 'These hundred things I dabble with.' "

Such an attitude of intense concentration involves "forgetting what lies behind." A runner who looks backward while running forward puts himself in danger. In part, Paul meant that he put behind him past failures. Having confessed them to the Lord, he accepted forgiveness and pressed on. Paul could have been paralyzed by regrets for his persecution of the church or his arrogant, self-righteous Pharisaism, or perhaps his inadequacies as a Christian. We must learn from the past, but we cannot be controlled by it. In the same way, it is necessary to forget past achievements. Paul had many of these, as an evangelist, missionary, theologian, and church planter. His was a record filled with impressive accomplishments, but he was perceptive enough to realize the tendency to rest on one's laurels and to relax in self-satisfied complacency. Paul did not ignore the past or seek to obliterate it. Rather, he focused his energies on the future.

Frozen in statue in Vancouver's Empire Stadium is a

golden moment in sports history. The year 1954 marked the first time that any athlete had run a mile in less than four minutes, and the British Empire games in Vancouver brought together the only two men who had accomplished a feat long thought impossible: Roger Bannister of England and John Landy of Australia. Landy led nearly all the way in a race billed as the Miracle Mile, but in the last turn he turned his head to locate Bannister. He broke stride slightly and, at that moment, Bannister passed him on the other shoulder and raced to victory. That moment has been captured by the sculptor—one man looking back while the other pressed on. I was a young boy listening to the race and I never fail to recall that moment as I read these words of Paul. He lived his life "reaching forward to what lies ahead" (Phil. 3:13). Like a runner straining to reach the finish line, he lived with an all-absorbing determination to lay hold of God's purpose for his life. There was nothing casual about Paul's attitude toward life!

HIS CONTROLLING COMMITMENT. Paul continues his athletic metaphor by designating the reason he strains toward the finish line: "the prize of the upward call of God in Christ Jesus" (Phil. 3:14). In the Greek games, the winner would be summoned to the judge's elevated stand to receive the wreath which the champion wore with pride, the ancient equivalent of a gold medal. Likewise, the Christian will be called into the presence of his Lord at the Rapture and will be summoned to the seat of the Judge (2 Cor. 5:10).

Paul's desire was to know the approval of his Lord. He valued the prize not so much for its intrinsic worth, but as a symbol of the Lord's approval of the service he lovingly had given. He knew that the only evaluation of his life and ministry which ultimately mattered was that of his Lord's; therefore, he directed his entire life toward the time when he stood before Him.

There is a price to be paid for such concentration. There were things Paul did not do, not because they were wrong, but because they were not consistent with his goal. There was undoubtedly criticism from those less motivated, which took its toll since Paul was not made of stone. But since there was perfect consistency between God's goal for his life and his personal goals, he was willing to pay the price of single-mindedness.

THE COST OF CONTINUATION

Waterman and and Peters, in their helpful study of excellence in business, conclude that "the excellent companies are, above all else, brilliant on the basics."[4] In Philippians 3:15-16, Paul indicates that the attitudes he has described in himself are attitudes basic to excellence. It is part of the mindset of maturity. Though Paul has denied in verse 12 that he has already reached maturity or perfection, he here speaks of those who are mature, or perfect. He is not contradicting himself but rather using the terms in two senses. In its absolute sense, Christian maturity awaits the Rapture, but in contexts such as verse 15, it describes relative Christian maturity.

Mature believers ought to think as Paul does. Indeed, Paul is confident that "if in anything you think differently, God will reveal even this to you." What's more, a believer can be confident that God will guide him, through the indwelling Spirit, and convict him of those areas inconsistent with the divine goal. When spiritual growth is the commitment of the believer, spiritual guidance is the promise to the believer. "Where there is a willingness to be taught of God, the illuminating grace of the Holy Spirit can be depended upon to open up His Word, and guide into all truth."[5]

However, the mature believer is not only to be confident about the future and committed to spiritual progress. Until future guidance comes, the instruction of Philippians 3:16 applies: "Let us keep living to that same standard to which we have attained." Mature believers have attained to a particular standard or principle of life which has brought them to their present level of maturity. In other words, Paul is indicating that disciplined continuance is the key to Christian maturity. He uses a word that suggests taking one step at a time in routine faithfulness, doing the will of God. There is nothing very dramatic about such a life but, as Hudson Taylor observed, "A man can be spiritually consecrated and dedicated and of very little use to God because his life is not disciplined." The consistent practice of God's principles of growth and the disciplined development of habits of holiness are indispensable to excellence. The principle applies in any sphere of endeavor. The athlete ceaselessly drills his fundamentals; the concert musician endlessly practices her exercises; the salesman rigorously perfects his techniques. Without discipline, there will be no excellence.

In recent times, jogging has become a national passion (some would say a disease). It's not hard to do, but it's very hard to keep doing, as many have learned when good intentions were sabotaged by sore muscles. In his book, *The Complete Book of Running*, the late James Fixx describes what he learned about the development of discipline:

> When we race, strange things happen to our minds. The stress of fatigue sometimes makes us forget why we wanted to race in the first place. In one of my early marathons I found myself unable to think of a single reason for continuing. Physically and mentally exhausted, I dropped out of the race. Now I won't enter a marathon unless I truly want to finish it. If during the race I can't remember why I wanted to run in it, I tell myself, "Maybe I can't remember now, but I know I had a good reason when I started." I've finally learned how to fight back when my brain starts using tricky arguments.[6]

The life of Paul is eloquent testimony to the fact that excellence is experienced only by those willing to pay the price. His choice of the goal of "the surpassing value of knowing Christ" is the choice essential to all true excellence. Man was made for God and to know Him is life's central privilege and its central power. Pursuing that goal is the heart of excellence, but it also involves setting aside all lesser values.

Excellence also involves the recognition that God has a purpose for every individual, a purpose that includes the common destiny of Christlikeness as well as a personal call to ministry. Though God does not reveal His individual purpose for the Christian in the same way He did to Paul, there is no reason to deny that such a purpose exists. The circumstances of life, the instructions of the Word, the counsel of others, the recognition of talents and gifts all combine to give insight into God's purpose for the individual.

There is also the cost of continuance: the disciplined, daily pursuit of one's goals. Excellence is not achieved by spectacular outbursts of energy or by grand efforts. It is in the daily grind of obedience and routine faithfulness to divine responsibilities that excellence is acquired.

CHAPTER NINE

THE PARADOX OF EXCELLENCE

Few things in life are more difficult to obtain than balance. A tendency to go to extremes seems inherent in human nature and theological considerations seem to arouse the habit in particularly virulent forms. The ancient controversy over divine sovereignty and human responsibility reflects this polarizing of positions, which divorces aspects of truth which God has bound together. Biblical truth often requires holding in tension apparently contradictory concepts which are in fact mutually dependent.

The biblical concept of excellence insists that human effort is indispensable in the pursuit of excellence. Rigorous self-discipline and a tenacious dedication to realize God's goals for one's life are essential to character-building and to the development of gifts and abilities. Apart from a high human motivation, mediocrity is inevitable. Yet there is a very real danger that the desire for excellence will degenerate into perfectionism. Many people are bound in a tyranny of obligations, feeling guilty because of their shortcomings, fearful of failure, and compulsively pursuing great achievements.

Therefore, God's Word also teaches that human effort is inadequate. The most highly motivated individual will fall far short of realizing God's purpose for his life, even if his efforts take him to the very limits of personal achievement in a particular sphere of endeavor. Because God's purpose will only be achieved at the Rapture, the most an individual can hope to achieve is a relative level of excellence, and he will be tempted to measure such excellence almost purely in terms of external achievements. Under such conditions, discouragement or self-deception flourishes. We either become acutely aware of our shortcomings or proudly misled by our contributions. The trap of perfectionism snares the self-sufficient pursuer of excellence, with his endless supply of success slogans and positive mental attitudes.

At its heart, then, the biblical concept of excellence contains a paradox because of the way it speaks of human effort and inadequacy. When, during World War II, the Russians suddenly announced a treaty with their bitterest enemy, Adolf Hitler, the world was astonished. It seemed impossible that Nazis and Communists could make common cause. Winston Churchill's words in Parliament were typically Churchillian: "I cannot forecast to you the action of Russia. It is a riddle wrapped in a mystery inside an enigma." The same terminology could be applied to a key truth of Christian living, though God's grace transforms contradictory components into complementary ones. In usual terminology, excellence involves maximizing human potential and achieving new levels of adequacy. However, in biblical terms, excellence is not the elimination of human inadequacy, but the divine empowerment of inadequate people.

Because biblical excellence primarily involves Christlikeness of character, it cannot be achieved by unaided human effort. One of the great contributions of the New Testament is to enable believers to be entirely realistic about human inadequacy and overwhelmingly confident of God's total adequacy. The paradox of excellence is that the Fall has rendered full human excellence unobtainable, and thus the recognition of human inadequacy is the prerequisite for experiencing God's adequacy. The indwelling enablement of the Holy Spirit means that the pursuit of excellence is neither futile nor fruitless, for His presence makes possible increasing conformity to Christ and continuing development of gifts. This confidence in God's work, however, is not a substitute for human energy, but an indispensable ally of it.

In His allegory of the Vine and the branches recorded in John 15, the Lord Jesus established the fundamental New Testament teaching about spiritual fruitfulness. Believers can produce fruit only as they abide in Christ, for apart from Him they can accomplish nothing of lasting value. The affirmation, "Apart from Me, you can do nothing," is obviously not a denial of human activity, but rather a denial that spiritual excellence is possible apart from constant fellowship with the Lord Jesus. The Christian life is thus lived on the basis of divine enablement rather than legalistic effort, a concept so central to the believer's life under grace that it can appropriately be termed *the* New Covenant principle. The major exposition of New Covenant living is 2 Corinthians 2:14—7:1, and though the entire passage has great significance, a section of particular importance to the biblical doctrine of excellence occurs in 4:7-18. This provides an essential counterbalance to those passages which emphasize the necessity of human activity in the pursuit of excellence.

The idea which pervades Paul's second letter to the Corinthians is that external appearances often distort inner reality. Coming under attack by opponents in Corinth because of his apparent vacillation in his relations with them (chapters 1—2), and because his personal appearance and style fell far short of that of some self-proclaimed apostles (chapters 10—13), Paul responds by directing his readers to the profound contrast between the external and temporal standards of the Old Covenant and the internal and external dimensions of the New Covenant. The former requires human activity; the latter promises divine sufficiency. The former demands human adequacy; the latter accepts human weakness. The former is based on confidence in man; the latter on confidence in God. The former demands success; the latter survives in suffering. Paul summarizes this principle in two memorable passages. The first is 2 Corinthians 3:4-6:

> And such confidence we have through Christ toward God. Not that we are adequate in ourselves to consider anything as coming from ourselves, but our adequacy is from God, who also made us adequate as servants of a new covenant, not of the letter, but of the Spirit; for the letter kills, but the Spirit gives life.

The second passage follows Paul's acknowledgment that he had three times petitioned the Lord to remove the mysterious thorn in the flesh which God had permitted Satan to inflict on him:

> And He has said to me, "My grace is sufficient for you, for power is perfected in weakness." Most gladly, therefore, I will rather boast about my weaknesses, that the power of Christ may dwell in me. Therefore I am well content with weaknesses, with insults, with distresses, with persecutions, with difficulties, for Christ's sake: for when I am weak then I am strong (2 Cor. 12:9-10).

It would be hard to imagine words more contrary to typical human concepts of excellence. Yet Paul's teaching reflects the consistent biblical emphasis on the primacy of character as well as the fundamental New Covenant principle of excellence amidst weakness. In 2 Corinthians 4:7-18, Paul expounds that theme in more detail:

> But we have this treasure in earthen vessels, that the surpassing greatness of the power may be of God and not from ourselves; we are afflicted in every way, but not crushed; perplexed, but not despairing; persecuted, but not forsaken; struck down, but not destroyed; always carrying about in the body the dying of Jesus, that the life of Jesus also may be manifested in our body. For we who live are constantly being delivered over to death for Jesus' sake, that the life of Jesus also may be manifested in our mortal flesh. So death works in us, but life in you. But having the same spirit of faith, according to what is written, "I believe, therefore I spoke," we also believe, therefore also we speak; knowing that He who raised the Lord Jesus will raise us also with Jesus and will present us with you. For all things are for your sakes, that the grace which is spreading to more and more people may cause the giving of thanks to abound to the glory of God.
>
> Therefore we do not lose heart, but though our outer man is decaying, yet our inner man is being renewed day by day. For momentary, light affliction is producing for us an eternal weight of glory far beyond all comparison, while we look not at the things which are seen, but at the things which are not seen; for the things

which are seen are temporal, but the things which are not seen are eternal.

GOD'S POWER AND HUMAN WEAKNESS

"No person was ever more aware of the paradoxical nature of Christianity than Paul. And perhaps none of his epistles contains more paradoxes than 2 Corinthians. With their numerous paradoxes, then, verses 7 to 12 [of 2 Corinthians 4] are typical of this epistle and of Paul's style."[1]

The series of paradoxes actually extends to verse 18 and falls into three major groupings. The first, found in verse 7, concerns the profound difference between the indescribable value of the treasure possessed by the believer and the apparent worthlessness of the container. It is a paradox built on three elements: the treasure, the container, and the purpose of God.

THE TREASURE. "We have this treasure," writes Paul. While the first person refers particularly to Paul in this context, it specifically includes all believers. The privilege of the New Covenant is the common possession of all believers, as Paul clearly indicates in 2 Corinthians 3:12-18. While the Old Covenant reserved access to the privileged few, in the New Covenant "we all, with unveiled face beholding as in a mirror the glory of the Lord, are being transformed into the same image from glory to glory, just as from the Lord, the Spirit" (3:18). Since there is no privileged caste in the New Covenant, all believers alike possess "this ministry" (4:1) and "this treasure" (4:7).

The treasure which we possess embraces the entirety of our New Covenant privileges. The heart of that privilege is beholding the glory of God in the face of Jesus Christ. Closely related to it is the privilege of being a servant of the New Covenant, possessing the responsibility to spread the knowledge of our Lord. The treasure, therefore, includes a message, but above all, it means that we know the Lord of the message: "Christ Himself, in whom are hidden all the treasures of wisdom and knowledge" (Col. 2:2-3). No higher treasure can be imagined than this!

THE CONTAINER. The amazing thing is that the treasure is contained "in earthen vessels." There was nothing fancy about such vessels. They were simple clay pots used commonly and extensively in the first century. Even today, the tourist shops of the Middle East are filled with such pots. They were the peanut butter jars of Paul's time—cheap, disposable, and fragile. The treasure is not found in fine china or expensive crystal, but in clay pots.

Paul is obviously describing our human bodies, but he is not suggesting that our bodies are worthless. His intention is rather to depict our weakness. Intrinsically, we are unworthy of the fine treasure we contain, just as a peanut butter jar is an inappropriate container for a multifaceted diamond. Paul wants us to recognize that our excellence is not what we are but what we contain. There is a liberating power in the recognition that the Lord does not ask me to be more than a clay pot. Therefore, I am able to live with a realistic appraisal of my personal limitations and liabilities, realizing that human nature at its very best is weak. This, of course, does not permit me to condone my sin but it does cause me to realize that I am only a container. At the same time, the danger is that I forget that true value is found in the treasure, not the pot, and as a result, seek to preserve the pot and hide God's treasure.

THE PURPOSE. This awesome contrast between treasure and container is not a mistake, but rather a result of the purpose of God. Human weakness is not a barrier to the display of God's power. On the contrary, human weakness provides the background against which the power of God is more clearly seen. When the Lord chooses to manifest His power through human frailty, there can be no doubt that "the surpassing greatness of the power [is] of God and not from ourselves" (2 Cor. 4:7). By using the word *surpassing*, Paul emphasizes that God's power does not merely match human weakness, but completely transcends it. As Denney eloquently observes:

No one who saw the exceeding greatness of the power which the Gospel exercised—not only in sustaining its preachers under persecution, but in transforming human nature, and making bad men good—no one who saw this, and looked at a preacher like Paul, could dream that the explanation lay in *him*. Not in an ugly little Jew, without eloquence, without presence, without the means to bribe or to compel, could the source of such courage, the cause of such transformations, be found; it must be sought, not in him, but in God.[2]

The implications of this paradox for the concept of excellence is immense. Because God's indwelling power supersedes human weakness, human excellence cannot be understood only in terms of either character or ability. Transcending both is availability as a channel of God's power. His enabling presence is able to transform people of mediocre gifts into individuals with outstanding impact. As a result, even the weakest of men can aspire to excellence through the enabling Spirit. As Hughes comments:

It is precisely the Christian's utter frailty which lays him open to the experience of the all-sufficiency of God's grace, so that he is even able to rejoice because of his weakness (2 Cor. 12:9ff)—something that astonishes and baffles the world, which thinks only in terms of human ability.[3]

If the New Covenant principle inspires hope in the discouraged believer, it ought also to bring humility to the self-important believer. No matter how impressive our gifts may be, we are never more than clay pots; true excellence lies in the treasure, not in the pot. We would be less than honest to deny that there is a natural human desire to protect and glorify the clay vessel, but to do so is to hide the treasure and to thwart divine power.

Denney warns of the danger of such a misplaced sense of confidence:

There have always been men in the world so clever that God could make no use of them; they could never do His work, because they were so lost in admiration of their own. But God's work never depended on them, and it does not depend on them now. It depends on those who, when they see Jesus Christ, become unconscious, once and forever, of all that they have been used to call their own wisdom and their strength. . . . The supreme law of [the kingdom] is still the glory of God, and not the glory of the clever men.[4]

THE PARADOX OF EXCELLENCE

CHRIST'S LIFE AND HUMAN SUFFERING

At the end of a tour of the United States in 1963, Helmut Thielicke, the distinguished German preacher-theologian, was interviewed by a group of journalists and theological students. One of those present at the press conference asked Thielicke what he considered to be the most important question of that time for Americans. His carefully measured answer is just as relevant now as it was then, particularly in a discussion of excellence:

> I would rather—if you will permit me to make a judgment—mention an entirely different problem as being the most important question which you are facing. Not a single person ever raised it in any discussion I had in this country (it would therefore appear that people are astonishingly unconscious of it); and whenever I raised it myself, it seemed to evoke a kind of disconcerted amazement, I might almost say, a kind of embarrassment, which was probably the reason why nobody ever broached the subject. I mean the question of how Americans deal with suffering. Yes, you have heard aright; I mean the problem of suffering. If I have not been totally blind on this journey, I believe I have seen that Americans do not have this color on their otherwise so richly furnished palette. . . .
>
> Again and again I have the feeling that suffering is regarded as something which is fundamentally inadmissible, distressing, embarrassing, and not to be endured. Naturally, we are called upon to combat and diminish suffering. All medical and social action is motivated by the perfectly justified passion for this goal. But the idea that suffering is a burden which can or even should be fundamentally radically exterminated can only lead to disastrous illusions. One perhaps does not even have to be a Christian to know that suffering belongs to the very nature of this our world and will not pass away until this world passes away. And beyond this, we Christians know that in a hidden way it is connected with man's reaching for the forbidden fruit, but that God can transform even this burden of a fallen world into a blessing and fill it with meaning.[5]

119

Paul's affirmation that divine power is at work in humanly weak vessels may give the false impression that he lives on a plane above human problems and difficulties. Exactly the opposite is, in fact, the case. External observations of Paul's life reveals an embattled sufferer dealing with overwhelming circumstances. But closer observation reveals that God's power is at work to prevent those circumstances from overwhelming him. The paradox is that God's power sustains the believer in suffering and weakness rather than delivering him from it. The believer, through Christ, is anything but a prisoner of his circumstances. Hughes summarizes Paul's message as follows:

> To be at the end of man's resources is not to be at the end of God's resources; on the contrary, it is to be precisely in the position best suited to prove and benefit from them, and to experience the surplus of the power of God breaking through and resolving the human difference.[6]

EXTERNAL DISTRESS, INNER DELIVERANCE. The apostle designates four realities of his constant experience which display the difference between his personal weakness and God's continual provision. Paul was not exempt from the difficulties of life, which he describes as pressure, perplexity, persecution, and catastrophe. But in every circumstance, God's enablement corresponded to Paul's need.

When Paul writes, "We are afflicted in every way," he uses a word which describes being under stress or pressure. His experience of it was constant and unremitting. Though the sources of his stress were unique, his experiences of it were not. It has been suggested that up to 70 percent of visits to family doctors are stress-related. It is important to notice Paul's response. He was not crushed, because the pressure was met by the internal power of the Holy Spirit. The answer to stress is not ultimately to fight it or flee it or flow with it, but rather to know the internal buttress supplied through fellowship with God's Spirit.

Paul also experienced perplexity. It is striking to hear the great apostle speak of himself as uncertain and confused, at a loss about the future. In 2 Corinthians 7:5-6, he describes such a time, when he felt overwhelmed. But to come to wit's end is not to come to hope's end. Because of his Lord's indwelling presence, he did not despair. There is a play on words in the Greek text which indicates that he never lost confidence in God's divine guidance even in the most confusing of circumstances.

Paul also experienced persecution: opposition from those hostile to his service for his Lord. Persecution takes many forms and results not only in the bloody martyrdom of a missionary, but also in the stalled career of a believer unwilling to compromise his integrity in business, or in a homemaker experiencing criticism because she will not jump on a feminist bandwagon. But no matter how fierce the opposition, Paul knew that he was never abandoned by his ever-faithful Lord.

Paul also experienced catastrophe; times when he was "knocked down" by overwhelming problems or unavoidable circumstances, such as he describes in 2 Corinthians 11:23-28. At such times, we are tempted to argue, as one best-selling author does, that bad things happen to good people because God is limited in His control. Paul's perception is entirely different. He knew that God's sovereignty meant that he would never be knocked out, even though, like Job, he might never know God's purpose in what He permits.

Second Corinthians 4:8-9 thus makes it very clear that the believer is not immune to the harsh realities of life. But neither is he imprisoned by them. The indwelling presence of God's Spirit brings transforming power to every experience of life. But God's purpose is to do more than sustain believers in suffering, and Paul indicates that purpose in verses 10-12.

LIFE SEEN IN DEATH. Second Corinthians 4:10 serves to introduce the basic principle demonstrated in Paul's experience. The suffering Paul experienced was directly related to the suffering the Lord Jesus experienced in His life. Paul describes his experiences of verses 8-9 as "always carrying about in the body the dying of Jesus" (v. 10). The particular word Paul uses when he speaks of the *dying* rather than the *death* of Jesus suggests that he is thinking not of the event of the Lord's death so much as the process of His self-giving and suffering for others, which culminated in His crucifixion. In other words, Paul is not speaking of our co-crucifixion with Christ, as he does in Romans 6, but rather of "that daily exposure to danger and death for His sake which constitutes [our] share in

His sufferings.'"[7] Tasker elaborates on Paul's description of "the dying of Jesus" as follows:

> As Paul well knew, Jesus had to spend much physical strength and spiritual energy in the service of others; He was relentlessly hunted down by His political and religious opponents; He experienced sleepless nights and exhausting days with nowhere to lay His head. It might indeed be said that the death that He ultimately died was but the final stage of a *dying* that had been continuous while He trod the way of obedience as the Suffering Servant of God.[8]

This identification with Christ's *dying* is so that "the life of Jesus also may be manifested in our body" (v. 10). The life of Jesus is the resurrection reality which Paul has described in verses 8-9, the divine power which transforms apparent defeat into ultimate victory. The weakness of the clay pot only serves to reveal more clearly the glory of the treasure! Paul reiterates the concept in verses 11-12 to highlight the paradox of the Christian life. Death and life are simultaneously at work in the believer's experience. Under the pressure of suffering, the inner quality of Christ's life is revealed, and thus his experience becomes a source of life and encouragement to others who observe, because they reveal the risen power of the risen Lord.

The most important word Paul uses is *manifested* (vv. 10-11). The life of Christ is present in every believer, but that life is revealed to others when the clay vessel is "broken" so that the inner treasure is exposed. Our natural instinct is to preserve the pot; God's purpose is to display the treasure. Therefore, the difficulties and sufferings do not threaten the believer's relationship with the Lord. On the contrary, such hardships provide an opportunity to manifest the indwelling life of Christ. An important precaution is implicit in Paul's words. Skills and talents can be used in such a way that it is the human container which is praised and exalted. But true excellence centers on the treasure. When the spotlight falls on the earthen vessel, man-centered skills and talents actually become the enemy of true excellence; suffering and weakness, on the other hand, can become its ally.

CONFIDENCE IN SUFFERING. While suffering is therefore an

inevitable and important aspect of Christian living, the believer is not a fatalist. The resurrection of the Lord Jesus brings confidence that suffering is not final, but will be swallowed up with triumph at the Rapture (v. 14). Furthermore, suffering is not meaningless, since it advances the Gospel and contributes to the greater glory of God (v. 15). Since the ultimate purpose of man is to glorify God, human weakness which manifests the life of Christ thus becomes a unique form of Christian excellence. Since it is far more important to manifest Christ than to display skills, Christians whom God calls on to endure suffering need to recognize their circumstances as a special means of achieving true excellence. The very handicaps and restrictions which seem, from the human perspective, to destroy all hope of excellence, can become the channels God uses. God's choicest saints have often been developed in the school of pain, and who can doubt that a Joni Eareckson Tada or a Kim Wickes display excellence in an undeniable and powerful way?

DIVINE ETERNITY AND HUMAN MORTALITY

The third paradox Paul develops also concerns the weakness and frailty of the human vessel, but this time the divine response is the permanence of the believer because of the indwelling Spirit and the hope of the resurrection. Decay and suffering may be an essential part of our present experience but they are not the ultimate truth about a believer's life. As Howard Hendricks loves to remind us, we are not in the land of the living on the way to the land of the dying. Because of the Saviour, we are in the land of the dying on our way to the land of the living. We are made for eternity.

PRESENT DECAY AND PERMANENT RENEWAL. Our outer person, our bodies, are subject to the universal law of decay. All that is mortal gradually experiences the corruption of time. But the believer, by regeneration, has an inner man possessed of an entirely different nature. The *inner man* is a term used by Paul in Romans 7:22 and Ephesians 3:16 to describe the new man in Christ. The outer man decays, but this eternal self is being daily renewed by the Holy Spirit into the image of Christ (Col. 3:10). Thus two processes operate simultaneously in the believer—physical decay and spiritual renewal. In the deepest sense, we are not getting older, we're getting better. As Denney observes:

The decay of the outward man in the godless is a melancholy spectacle, for it is the decay of everything; in the Christian, it does not touch that life which is hid with Christ in God, and which is in the soul itself a well of water springing up to eternal life.[9]

PRESENT AFFLICTION AND ETERNAL REWARD. The present is not only a time of decay, but a time of suffering and affliction. When Paul speaks of our "momentary, light affliction" (2 Cor. 4:17), he is not suggesting that our sufferings are trivial or insignificant. His own afflictions were intense and unrelenting. But compared to the eternal glory which is God's reward for the believer, those afflictions were as nothing. The present suffering, by God's grace, is producing a disproportional eternal reward, one which is far beyond all comparison to our present difficulties and quite beyond all human conception. As Paul indicates in Romans 8:18, "The sufferings of this present time are not worthy to be compared to the glory that is to be revealed to us." In the midst of our troubles they seem unrelenting and unpassing. In fact, they are short-lived, especially in comparison with eternity. Eternity alone is permanent. Our afflictions seem heavy and weighty, but God wants us to realize that it is His eternal glory which has substance.

PRESENT APPEARANCE AND ETERNAL REALITY. Paul's final word is to remind us that the believer sees life entirely differently than the natural man. The natural man focuses on the visible and is convinced that it represents the permanent. Therefore, he believes that excellence lies in the realm of the tangible and is measured by appearances and pragmatic standards. The believer views life through the eyes of faith. He therefore focuses on "the things which are not seen" which are eternal, since they are related to the glory of God, and evaluates excellence in those terms. That which is impressive but purely temporary cannot properly be considered excellent. This has tremendous implications for our understanding of excellence. Whatever we do which has no implications for eternity cannot be truly excellent. The fading wreath of human achievement pales beside the unfading wreath of eternal things (1 Cor. 9:25). Nowhere is that more clearly seen than at a funeral. It is amazing how irrelevant many activities and achievements seem when measured by eternity! But all of life can be related to eternal things, and thus take the character of true excellence.

The perspective of the New Covenant is indispensable to a biblical concept of excellence. The natural tendency is to define excellence in terms of the external. The impressive "vessel" and the highly visible performance are the epitome of excellence as it is usually defined.

The New Covenant emphasizes the internal and the eternal. Human weakness is not an enemy to excellence when there is dependence on the Holy Spirit. Excellence for a believer can be understood only in relation to the power of God and the glory of God. As the power of God transcends the limitations of human frailty, God's purpose for the believer is realized and true excellence is achieved.

In her fascinating children's story, *The Velveteen Rabbit*, Margery Williams tells of a stuffed toy rabbit which is given as a Christmas present. Prized for a few moments, it is soon discarded for more exciting toys and then finds itself becoming a friend of an old veteran of the nursery, the Skin Horse.

The Skin Horse had lived longer in the nursery than any of the others. He was so old that his brown coat was bald in patches and showed the seams underneath, and most of the hairs in his tail had been pulled out to string bead necklaces. He was wise, for he had seen a long succession of mechanical toys arrive to boast and swagger, and by-and-by break their mainsprings and pass away, and he knew that they were only toys, and would never turn into anything else. For nursery magic is very strange and wonderful, and only those playthings that are old and wise and experienced like the Skin Horse understand all about it.

"What is Real?" asked the Rabbit one day, when they were lying side by side near the nursery fender, before Nana came to tidy the room. "Does it mean having things that buzz inside you and a stick-out handle?"

"Real isn't how you are made," said the Skin Horse. "It's a thing that happens to you. When a child loves you for a long, long time, not just to play with, but *really* loves you, then you become Real."

"Does it hurt?" asked the Rabbit.

"Sometimes," said the Skin Horse, for he was always truthful. "When you are Real you don't mind being hurt."

"Does it happen all at once, like being wound up," he asked, "or bit by bit?"

"It doesn't happen all at once," said the Skin Horse. "You become. It takes a long time. That's why it doesn't often happen to people who break easily, or have sharp edges, or who have to be carefully kept. Generally, by the time you are Real, most of your hair has been loved off, and your eyes drop out and you get loose in the joints and very shabby. But these things don't matter at all, because once you are Real you can't be ugly, except to people who don't understand."[10]

God's excellence lives in a world of reality and frees us to be authentic men and women. The New Covenant calls us to realize that we are only clay pots, and excellence involves the manifestation of God's indwelling treasure, as a demonstration of His surpassing power. The paradox of excellence is that, as we recognize our inadequacies, we are able to learn the truth of Christ's complete sufficiency.

CHAPTER TEN

THE CLIMATE OF EXCELLENCE

Excellence is infectious. It flourishes in a context where it is modeled, expected, and nurtured. A personal commitment to pursue excellence for the glory of God is indispensable. But biblical excellence is not individualistic. There is both a corporate form of excellence and a corporate climate in which excellence is best fostered. The Head of the church has a purpose for His people, and in moving toward that goal, the church is moving toward excellence. In so doing, it inspires believers within it to pursue excellence in their own lives.

The importance of a climate of excellence is widely recognized. Certain athletic teams are notable for their consistently high quality. Putting on the uniform seems to inspire an athlete to perform at the very limits of his ability. Peters and Waterman have observed the powerful effects of a company's "culture" on its employees. "The excellent companies," they conclude, "are marked by very strong cultures, so strong that you either buy into their norms or get out."[1] These cultures not only determine production, they provide motivation. The set of shared values, procedures, and goals which guides the company not only guides company policy, but also provides a family identity which gives people a sense of purpose and mission. "The institution provides guiding belief and creates a sense of excitement, a sense of being a part of the best, a sense of producing something of quality that is generally valued."[2] Peters and Waterman contend that excellent companies have an intensity of commitment to their values that is contagious, so that they "require and demand extraordinary performance from the average man."[3] This commitment to seek the best is epitomized in the observation of a consumer goods chief executive officer:

> We have slowly discovered that our most effective goal is to be *the best* at certain things. We now try to get our people to help work out what these things should be, how to define *best* objectively, and how to become best in our selected spheres. You would be surprised at how motivating that can be.[4]

Gardner has also described the powerful effects of a climate of excellence on an individual. Motivation to excellence is not purely personal. As he observes:

> The degree of motivation which an individual possesses at any given time is very much affected by what is expected (or demanded) of him. . . .
> We all know that some organizations, some families, some athletic teams, some political groups inspire their members to great heights of personal performances. In other words, high individual performance will depend to some extent on the capacity of the society or institution to evolve it. And woe to the society that loses the gift for such evocation! When an institution or nation loses its capacity to evoke high individual performance, its great days are over.[5]

It is common to minimize the importance of social environment to excellence, whether of character or of performance. Many illustrations of excellence take a classic "man against immense odds" form. The Horatio Alger legend does provide valuable motivation to attack difficult circumstances, but it is misleading if taken as the norm of excellence. As Gardner further observes:

> We are beginning to understand that the various kinds of talent that flower in any society are the kinds that are valued in the society. . . .

More and more we are coming to see that high performance, particularly where children are concerned, takes place in a framework of expectation. If it is expected it will often occur. If there are no expectations, there will be little high performance.[6]

Writing from a very different perspective, but observing the same principle of contagious standards, Hyde describes the powerful appeal of the Communist Party. As he states, "They believe that if you make big demands upon people you will get a big response."[7] Communists' definition of excellence bears little resemblance to the biblical one, but they do clearly perceive the importance of a corporate support group to fostering it. Hyde describes the process as follows:

Like attracts like. Those who are attracted by the dedication they see within the movement will themselves be possessed of a latent idealism, a capacity for dedication. Thus dedication perpetuates itself. It sets the tone and pace of the movement as a whole. This being so, the movement can make big demands upon its followers, knowing that the response will come. If the majority of members of an organization are halfhearted and largely inactive, then it is not surprising if others who join it soon conform to the general pattern. If the organization makes relatively few demands upon its members and if they quite obviously feel under no obligation to give a very great deal to it, then those who join may be forgiven for supposing that this is the norm and that this is what membership entails.

If, on the other hand, the majority of members, from the leaders down, are characterized by their single-minded devotion to the cause, if it is quite clear that the majority are giving until it hurts, putting their time, money, thought, and if necessary life itself at its disposal, then those who consider joining will assume that this is what will be expected of them. If they nonetheless make the decision to join, they will come already conditioned to sacrifice till it hurts.

It is ludicrous to suppose that halfhearted Christians can conduct a fruitful dialogue with fully dedicated

Communists. Perhaps it is this which underlies the fear of any such dialogue, felt by some Christians. They take it for granted that in any such dialogue the Communists must come out on top, that the Marxists will be the gainers, the Christians the losers. I would suggest that if this happens it will have less to do with Communist duplicity than with Communist dedication—although the Christian in such circumstances must be prepared for the duplicity too. The well-instructed, fully committed, totally dedicated Christian has little to fear. But dedication must be met with dedication.[8]

This all has obvious importance to the church of Jesus Christ. By its very nature, the church is a corporate entity with a corporate destiny and a corporate purpose. God not only calls individual Christians to excellence, He calls local churches to excellence. The New Testament depicts the church as the means by which God's manifold wisdom is being showcased to heavenly beings (Eph. 3:10), and the local church as a "pillar and support of the truth" (1 Tim. 3:15). It is together that "we all attain to the unity of the faith, and of the knowledge of the Son of God, to a mature man, to the measure of the stature which belongs to the fullness of Christ" (Eph. 4:13).

The church ought, therefore, to be an organization that fosters excellence, calling believers, individually and collectively, to the pursuit of excellence. A congregation ought to be a catalyst for mutual growth, providing a context in which every Christian is challenged to maturity, encouraged in his growth, and equipped with the required nutrients. In this way, the local church also provides what Guinness has described as the "plausibility structure" for the Gospel, since "the church is Christianity's working model, its pilot plant, its future in embryo."[9]

That excellence is the standard for the church is clear from Paul's exhortation to the Thessalonian believers (1 Thes. 4:1, 10) to "excel still more." The early Christians outlived, outthought, and outdied their contemporaries. Many components are essential to establishing a climate of excellence, but probably the three most important are the concept of discipleship, the responsibility of leadership, and the mutual ministry of spiritual gifts.

THE SCHOOL OF DISCIPLESHIP

One of the chief contributions of the work of Peters and Waterman is their pervasive emphasis on the fact that excellent companies are intensely people-oriented. The same is true of excellent churches. They are committed to invest in people and specifically to obey the Great Commission by making disciples (Matt. 28:16-20). The call is not to make people *our* disciples but to make them disciples of the Lord Jesus. In fact, the term *disciple* in Acts is a synonym for *believer* (e.g., Acts. 6:1-2, 7; 9:1; 11:26, 29). The mark of a disciple is his personal relationship to the Lord. Jesus Christ is the only Teacher and Lord whose teaching is authoritative (Matt. 5:21-22) and whose authority is unquestioned (John 13:13). Disciples are people in training; the goal of their training is likeness to their Lord (Luke 6:40). Thus, disciples live with unrivaled and unquestioning devotion to their Saviour (Matt. 10:37-39; Luke 14:26ff).

The church, then, is not merely a collection of believers. It is a congregation of disciples. Ladd helpfully describes the distinctive nature of Christian discipleship:

Discipleship to Jesus was not like discipleship to a Jewish rabbi. The rabbis bound their disciples not to themselves but to the Torah; Jesus bound His disciples to Himself. The rabbis offered something outside of themselves; Jesus offered Himself alone. Jesus required His disciples to surrender without reservation to His authority. They thereby became not only disciples but also *douloi*, slaves (Matt. 10:24ff; Luke 12:35ff, 42ff). This relationship has no parallel in Judaism. Discipleship to Jesus involved far more than following in His retinue; it meant nothing less than complete personal commitment to Him and His message.[10]

The first mark of a disciple, therefore, is that he is personally related and unconditionally committed to Jesus Christ as his Lord and Master. As Coleman notes, "Jesus expected the men He was with to obey Him. They were not required to be smart, but they had to be loyal. This became the distinguishing mark by which they were known."[11] A disciple's relationship to the Lord is one of self-sacrificing surrender (Luke 14:25-35).

131

Second, a disciple lives his life under the authority of the Word of God. Jesus is his Teacher. "If you abide in My Word, then you are truly disciples of Mine" (John 8:31). A disciple is a person of the Word, obeying the Lord through the Scriptures, and in that obedience, finding freedom.

Third, a disciple is committed to fellow-disciples as an evidence of love for the Lord. "By this all men will know that you are My disciples, if you have love for one another" (John 13:35). A genuine disciple will be committed in love to others. One cannot be a disciple in isolation from the body. A primary evidence of love is a servant mentality to others, as the context of the Lord's words indicates (John 13:1-20).

Fourth, a disciple displays his faith-allegiance to the Lord by spiritual fruitfulness. "By this is My Father glorified, that you bear much fruit and so prove to be My disciples" (John 15:8). Fruit cannot be defined in any narrow way in this passage. *Fruit* is the visible expression of the life of the vine. Since fruit does not exist for the benefit of the branch, but for others, it probably represents a godly character which is evidenced through evangelism or edification. A believer proves to be a disciple through his ministry to others.

These qualities of a disciple suggest that discipling is the process of bringing a believer to complete submission, devotion, and service to the Lord Jesus. It involves moving Christians toward increasing maturity in Christ so that they become able to have a ministry in the lives of others, enabling them, in turn, to grow in maturity. It means helping a believer become dependent on and accountable to the Lord Jesus.

A church must constantly evaluate its effectiveness by whether or not it is making such disciples. Since this is the Lord's mandate *for* the church, it is also the measuring standard *of* the church. It is therefore important to develop a model of the disciple-making process. Seven factors are essential:

1. Discipling is a *maturing* process. The goal of Christian ministry is not simply to make converts, but to make disciples. A disciple is a maturing, committed follower of the Lord Jesus Himself, obedient to Him. It is of primary importance to a disciple that he lives in and under the Word of God. He therefore must know how to handle God's Word.

2. Discipling is a *modeling* process. It involves the wholehearted investment of one's life in the lives of others.

"We were well pleased to impart to you not only the Gospel but also our own lives, because you had become very dear to us" (1 Thes. 2:8). But the model must constantly point away from himself to the Lord Jesus. As Richards and Martin observe:

> In the New Testament portrait, *discipleship is not to an individual, but to Christ Himself.* Paul could say to the Corinthians, "Follow my example," but he had to put this exhortation into perspective by adding, "as I follow the example of Christ" (1 Cor. 11:1). Christ is being formed in the believer. It is the Christ in the mature believer whom the disciple is to follow.[12]

3. Discipling is a *mutual* process. It is in the context of the local church that disciples are formed, as different believers exercise their spirtiual gifts (Eph. 4:11-16). Discipling does not take place simply on a one-to-one basis. Even 2 Timothy 2:2, the slogan verse of one-on-one discipling, emphasizes the group nature of discipling: "The things which you have heard from me in the presence of *many witnesses,* these entrust to faithful men, who will be able to teach others also" (italics mine). A related concept is that discipling does not best take place in a teacher-student role, but in a brother-brother role, which constantly focuses on Christ. Even Paul speaks of being mutually encouraged by each other's faith (Rom. 1:11-12).

4. Discipling is a *multiple* process. It requires the input of many believers to make a disciple. That is an obvious corollary of the doctrine of spiritual gifts, as Paul indicates in Ephesians 4:11-16. Every believer who is faithfully exercising his gift in the body, to the glory of the Lord, is part of the discipling process. Discipling is also multiple in method. It requires individual input, group fellowship, public instruction, and corporate worship. These are the "all things" of Matthew 28:20 (KJV) which the early church practiced in Acts 2:41-42. Disciples are formed in a church with a healthy balance.

5. Discipleship is a *manifold* process. That is to say, it concerns every area of life. Evangelism and follow-up are only aspects of a godly life. The New Testament pattern is all of life brought under the lordship of Christ. To be a disciple means living for the Lord in the world, not just in the church.

6. Discipleship is a *ministry* process. A disciple will discover his own place of ministry in the body. But since the New Testament does not teach "cookie-cutter discipleship," the ministry of one individual will not simply reproduce that of another. Every disciple has a ministry, but not every disciple has the same ministry. Not even each of the Twelve served the Saviour in the same way. Therefore, we must not pour disciples into a precast mold and describe only specific activities as part of disciple-making. There are certain things all believers should do in their relationships with other believers (e.g., Rom. 12:9-21), but these cannot be stereotyped.

7. Discipleship is a *multiplying* process. As individuals come to maturity in Christ, their lives will in turn affect others at the point of their godly character and spiritual gifts. A solid core of disciples will see God's blessing quantitatively and qualitatively. Spectacular programs may swell attendance and even lengthen membership lists. But only discipleship will produce lasting fruit (John 15:16). This is dramatically illustrated in Revelation 2—3. There, two small assemblies growing in discipleship are commended by the Lord while other churches, larger and apparently experiencing faster numerical growth, receive divine condemnation. When the Lord looks at the church, He counts disciples, not converts and warm bodies.

THE VISION OF LEADERSHIP

If discipleship is the process whereby believers are moved toward maturity in Christ, leadership is the process by which values are shaped, vision is shared, and goals are achieved. An environment of excellence is never the product of chance or good fortune, but of effective leadership. The admission of Peters and Waterman is revealing:

> How did these companies get the way they are? Is it always a case of a strong leader at the helm? We must admit that our bias at the beginning was to discount the role of leadership heavily, if for no other reason than that everybody's answer to what's wrong (or right) with whatever organization is its leader. Our strong belief was that the excellent companies had gotten to be the way they are because of a unique set of cultural attributes that distinguish them from the rest, and if we understood

those attributes well enough, we could do more than just mutter "leadership" in response to questions like "Why is J & J so good?" Unfortunately, what we found was that associated with every excellent company was a strong leader (or two) who seemed to have had a lot to do with making the company excellent in the first place. . . . The role of the chief executive is to manage the values of the organization.[13]

In a perceptive comment describing mediocre institutions, Gardner writes, "Like the sand dunes in the desert, they are shaped by influences but not by purposes."[14] "Men," he observes, "become prisoners of their procedures. The rule book grows fatter as the ideas grow fewer."[15] A climate of excellence requires excellence of leadership—people who inspire vision and action. Without such direction, mediocrity is inevitable. As Burns laments:

One of the most universal cravings of our times is a hunger for creative and compelling leadership. . . . The crisis of leadership today is the mediocrity or irresponsibility of so many men and women in power, but leadership rarely rises to the full need of it.[16]

The local church cannot escape the importance of leadership. If it is truly to become a cradle of excellence, it will only be because leaders set the pace, establish clear values, and motivate others to pursue excellence with them.

David's generation was blessed by the presence of the sons of Issachar, "men who understood the times, with knowledge of what Israel should do" (1 Chron. 12:32). A more succinct description of capable leaders can scarcely be imagined. However, tomes have been written on the subject of leadership and it still remains an elusive quality. It is, however, possible to delineate a number of characteristics the New Testament depicts as essential qualities.

RESPONSIBILITY. A leader must be willing to accept his God-given responsibility, "not under compulsion, but voluntarily" (1 Peter 5:2). This means a recognition of divine appointment ("the Holy Spirit has made you overseers," Acts 20:28) as well as a commitment to be an active decision-maker, to be a catalyst and not merely a chameleon. The local church must be shaped by divine purposes, not merely by varied influences. It must be led by those who are optimistic and positive because they rely on God's Spirit.

INTEGRITY. The biblical leader commands respect by virtue of his character. He does not demand it due to his position. The great stress in the various lists of qualifications (1 Tim. 3:1-13; Titus 1:5-9) is on the leader's personal character, since biblical leaders lead by "proving to be examples to the flock" (1 Peter 5:3). In other words, God's leader is a model and a pacesetter.

INDUSTRY. Hard work is an essential of leadership. Therefore, leaders are described as "those who diligently labor among you" (1 Thes. 5:12), people who not only dream dreams, but who pay the price to make them come true. Perseverance and discipline are indispensable partners of this kind of industry.

VISION. Effective leadership requires a deep dissatisfaction with the status quo which is fed by an intense desire to carry out the unfulfilled task. The apostles' commitment was to devote themselves "to prayer, and to the ministry of the Word" (Acts 6:4). A related aspect of vision is a tough-minded commitment to see the problems of the present as well as the possibilities of the future. Gardner perceptively observes:

> Most ailing organizations have developed a functional blindness to their own defects. They are not suffering because they can't *solve* their problems but because they won't *see* their problems. They can look straight at their faults and rationalize them as virtues or necessities.[17]

CREATIVITY. Leaders need to be informed about the world with an itching desire to be relevant. This requires a commitment to be fixed in principles but flexible in form, in a people-oriented way. The apostles in Acts 6 model a commitment to adapt to a new problem by a creative, flexible structure. Drucker describes the importance of this quality when he writes:

> An organization which just perpetuates today's level of vision, excellence, and accomplishment has lost the ca

pacity to adapt. And since the one and only thing certain in human affairs is change, it will not be capable of survival in a changed tomorrow.[18]

UNITY. Effective leadership involves teamwork among leaders and stimulates involvement by followers. There must be a commitment to work together, "standing firm in one spirit, with one mind striving together for the faith of the Gospel" (Phil. 1:27).

STRATEGY. Leaders must be goal-oriented individuals who not only determine priorities but also develop procedures to reach them. Thus the apostles not only recognized what the Jerusalem congregation required, but worked out a pattern to accomplish their goals (Acts 6:3-4). Central to a biblical strategy of ministry is the concept of "equipping the saints for the work of service" (Eph. 4:12). This must involve the motivation of believers to realize God's purpose for their lives, which is an essential component of excellence. As Burns observes:

All leadership is goal-oriented. The failure to set goals is a sign of faltering leadership. Successful leadership points in a direction; it is also the vehicle of continuing and achieving purpose.[19]

THE MINISTRY OF SPIRITUAL GIFTS

Leaders ought to shape the values of a local congregation in a way that fosters disciple-making. A third essential component in a climate of excellence is the ministry of spiritual gifts, which is part of common participation in body life.

The most extensive description of the process of body life is found in Paul's exposition of it in 1 Corinthians 12. Having stressed the unity of believers in verses 12-13 based on their common position in Christ and their common possession of the Spirit, he confronts two issues which have direct bearing on a climate of excellence in a congregation. The entire chapter concerns the doctrine of spiritual gifts and its relation to the fact that the church is one body with many members. But gifts differ. Believers do not possess the same gifts nor are they gifted to the same degree. The way individuals respond to these differences is essential to the understanding and achievement of excellence.

The first possible response to diversity of gifts is discontent and dissatisfaction. Recognizing the relatively inferior nature of his gifts, an individual is tempted to feel discouraged and unneeded. The foot is less complex and less conspicuous than a hand, as is an ear compared to an eye. Both lack the functional importance and physical attractiveness of the "superior" part. In the same way, those with lesser spiritual gifts may seem less important. How can a person with secondary gifts achieve excellence?

Paul's answer is very straightforward. First, diversity is essential. "The body is not one member but many" (v. 14). As Morris observes, "Diversity is not an accidental attribute of the body. It is its very essence. No one member is to be equated with the body."[20] Second, diversity does not mean dispensability. The foot and ear are no less part of the body than the hand or eye. "The body is crippled when one member is not functioning. It can be at peak efficiency only when every single part is active."[21] To ignore one's own importance or to covet another's function is to deny the nature of the body. Third, diversity is of divine origin. "But now God has placed the members, each one of them, in the body, just as He desired" (v. 18). The function each believer has results from the sovereign purpose and loving wisdom of God. This gives immense dignity to every believer. He places each one where He desires and where He deems best.

The conclusion which must be drawn is that every believer has immense significance; he has both a personal form of excellence and a unique contribution to make to corporate excellence. The body is not excellent when each member does the same thing, but when each member functions according to divine design. Each gift has its own form of excellence and each believer must be challenged to seek it. The rich variety of potential within the body needs to be realized at all levels.

A second response to diversity of gifts is the exact opposite. While the less gifted are tempted to despise their own gifts and read themselves out of the body, the more obviously gifted are tempted to despise the gifts of others and to read them out of the body. The eye may feel that it is superior even to the highly complex and conspicuous hand and believe it needs nothing else. The temptation of the gifted is to overestimate their importance.

Paul makes it clear that such an attitude is nonsensical. Appearances are deceptive. "The members of the body which seem to be weaker are necessary" (v. 22). In fact, they are indispensable, as the word *necessary* suggests. The "weaker parts" of the human body, such as the internal organs, are also vital. Furthermore, the physical body teaches that the "less physically attractive" parts are those which receive special honor. Unattractive or private members are given honor and attention because of the recognition that dignity of appearance is not the same as dignity of function. In the same way, gifted members need to realize that God has "blended" the body as a great artist blends colors to produce a harmonious, attractive whole, "that there should be no division in the body, but that the members should have the same care for one another" (v. 25).

The interrelatedness of the body destroys the concept of individualistic excellence achieved in isolation from others. No member of the body of Christ is complete in himself. He is dependent on others to realize personal maturity. He is also responsible to others, to enable them to move toward excellence. Each is indispensable if the body is to display what the Lord intends. As every believer develops his gifts and potentialities to the maximum, the church becomes what its Head intends and equips it to be.

THE WITNESS OF EXCELLENCE

The New Testament thus recognizes that standards and values are contagious. The pursuit of excellence is not intended to be the lonely pursuit of the solitary aspirant. Rather, the stimulating ministry of believers to one another in the body should create an environment in which excellence is expected as well as nurtured.

An essential part of the early church's impact on the ancient world was the plausibility given the Gospel by the quality of their corporate lives. Belief and behavior were inextricably linked. As the Apostle Paul writes, "We have renounced the things hidden because of shame, not walking in craftiness or adulterating the Word of God, but by the manifestation of truth commending ourselves to every man's conscience in the sight of God" (2 Cor. 4:2).

The early apologists returned to this theme again and

again. When they were slandered by opponents, they pointed to their corporate life as the cradle of moral excellence. Thus, the second-century writer, Theophilus, refuted the charges made by opponents by pointing to the undeniable evidence of changed lives:

> Be it far from Christians to conceive any such deeds; for with them temperance dwells, self-restraint is practiced, monogamy observed, chastity guarded, righteousness exercised, worship performed, God acknowledged; truth governs them, grace guards them, peace screens them, and the holy Word guides them.[22]

Athenagoras speaks in similar words:

> Among us you will find uneducated persons and artisans, and old women who, if they are unable in words to prove the benefit of our doctrine, yet by their deeds exhibit the benefits arising from their persuasion of its truth. They do not practice speeches, but exhibit good works; when struck, they do not strike again; when robbed they do not go to law; they give to those that ask of them, and they love their neighbors as themselves.[23]

These local churches were not perfect, but such claims would have no weight had they been absurd fabrications.

Only when the church of Jesus Christ acts as a catalyst to moral and spiritual excellence does its witness have both credibility and plausibility. But when believers can speak, as did Athenagoras and Theophilus, in simple truth and not in wishful boasting, of the evident excellence of God's people, the message of the Gospel rings out with authentic power.

CHAPTER ELEVEN

PROBLEMS OF EXCELLENCE

Probably no biblical doctrine is without its problems. Some of these derive from the nature of the biblical revelation, which means that doctrinal statements are human constructs. The Scriptures do not answer all of the questions we ask. More often, problems arise because the biblical data is distorted or mishandled. Most commonly, biblical truths are not kept in proper balance and worldly assumptions are imposed on the Word.

The biblical concept of excellence is not without associated problems. Most of these are due to imposing a preconceived notion of excellence on the Scriptures rather than deriving the concept inductively from the Word. Four major problem areas are evident. One is a utilitarian concept of excellence which links it to success. A second problem is a relativistic approach to excellence, which results in comparison and competition. Third is an absolutist concept, which leads to perfectionism. A fourth problem concerns excellence as a motivational and inspirational concept, as it is used by proponents of positive mental attitude.

EXCELLENCE AND SUCCESS

The American dream is prosperity and success. Our culture is obsessed with the notion that the good life involves the fulfillment of one's sensual desires, thus the national preoccupation with physical health, popularity, prosperity, power, pleasure, and personal peace. Horatio Alger is not a remote fictional character so much as the embodiment of the American ideal.

To make the Gospel more desirable in a free enterprise society, theologies have been developed which claim to guarantee all the good things of life to believers. Consumer religion assures us that health, wealth, and prosperity are the believer's "God-given right." Slogans abound: "Name it and claim it"; "God wants you rich"; "Think mink"; "Go first class—you're a King's kid"; and so forth. Such ideas are enticing and market well, especially on television. The assumption is that spiritual excellence is causally related to worldly success. Believers can expect success, since the more prosperity the believer enjoys, the more glory the Lord receives.

However, such attempts to sanctify the American dream are possible only by distorting biblical revelation. Worldly success is evaluated only by the present, with no reference to the will of God or to eternity. But true spiritual excellence and success are built around the concepts of God's purpose for man and His program of time and eternity. The two are often in direct conflict, "for that which is highly esteemed among men is detestable in the sight of God" (Luke 16:15).

Grounds aptly observes that "the world judges a person from two perspectives: private enterprise and public impact."[1] Of these two, public impact is given higher value. A person who lives a morally impeccable and responsible life may be considered a failure if he makes no public impact. Yet a person who is famous for his public impact, even though his personal life is riddled with failures, will be considered a success. "Popularity, fame, influence, political power, rare creativity, enormous wealth—these mark the successful person."[2]

Obviously, such criteria are the reverse of the biblical order. The Word of God insists on the primacy of godly character. Indeed, worldly success is often very deceptive, since it has little to do with personal merit.

Inherited advantages and fortuitous circumstances play important roles. Success may also be delusory. What present circumstances proclaim to be success, the passage of time reveals to be dismal failure. Most important, success is due to divine providence. Why He elevates one and not another is hidden in the eternal counsels of God, but the determining factor is not invariably the godliness or personal excellence of individuals.

The Christian is to strive for success but he is not guaranteed worldly success or earthly rewards. Indeed, the results may be exactly the opposite. Joseph's moral excellence led to his imprisonment. Daniel's extraordinary spirit did not prevent his enemies' machinations against him. Few would have evaluated the Lord Jesus as a success on the day of His crucifixion, since He lacked all that the world considers essential. The list is endless. Hebrews 11 alone totally destroys the facile theology which promises health, wealth, and prosperity to the godly. The great unnamed host of men and women of faith would have found such promises strange indeed. Of them, we read, "They were stoned, they were sawn in two, they were tempted, they were put to death with the sword; they went about in sheepskins, in goatskins, being destitute, afflicted, ill-treated (men of whom the world was not worthy), wandering in deserts and mountains and caves and holes in the ground" (Heb. 11:37-38).

The Bible is not opposed to concepts of success, but it measures success in terms of God and eternity. This means that there is an inevitable conflict between spiritual excellence and worldly success. Often the believer will be forced to choose which of the two he desires, for, as the Saviour declares, "You cannot serve God and mammon" (Matt. 6:24). This is not to suggest that success is impossible for the Christian. The Lord graciously granted it to Joseph and Daniel, but neither was any less excellent when he was imprisoned than when he was in high office. The Lord graciously entrusted them with success, as He does to many of His people. But He never guarantees it.

Success, therefore, must not be taken as an evidence of excellence. Nor does true excellence guarantee worldly success. An individual of immense skills may never rise to the top, not because of his failure but because of his character. His unwillingness to compromise God's values or to play the required politics may make him unwelcome in the higher echelons of his profession. Or his commitment to be a whole person may make him unable to pursue a single goal with the intensity required. Faith in Christ is not a title deed to diamonds, dollars, and a corner office; the cross of Christ has not been gilded. The gospel of success is a distortion of the Gospel of grace.

One important measure of the truth of an idea is its transferability to other cultures and contexts. The biblical concept of excellence is transferable to a Third World context of suffering and deprivation. Even in such circumstances, a believer can pursue God's goals for his life. But the gospel of success only mocks faithful believers living under totalitarian regimes or suffering the agonies of starvation and disease. Guinness properly labels it "consumer religion": "religion shaped by the priorities and demands of the economic order."[3] Magliato terms it "the Wall Street gospel," and summarizes its major fallacies as follows:

> The Word of God is not opposed to prosperity. But we can be sure that God is more interested in the person behind the wheel than the make of the car being driven.
>
> To place material possessions in a prominent position not only incites greed but is as foreign to the New Testament as camels on Wall Street. Jesus said that a man's life does not consist in the abundance of possessions. To say that God "wills" material prosperity for all His children is to say that any child of God not enjoying prosperity is outside God's will and is living a Satan-defeated life. This is not biblical. . . .
>
> We have been victimized by our culture. The American obsession with success, shortcuts, and pleasure has created an Americanized Gospel—a perverted Gospel that teaches, "Ye shall know them by their Cadillacs." When we stand before the Holy Trinity, our possessions won't amount to a hill of beans, and the fruit that Jesus will be looking for will be the results of our obedience to His will. Jesus is Lord. I cannot make Him my servant.[4]

The equation of excellence and success is not only false, it is dangerous, as Bulle has pointed out. She writes:

> The deception in the success-prosperity doctrine is subtle. It sounds so spiritual to assert that we cannot be sick or fail if we trust God, and that He will reward us for faith and giving and being good by making us rich in

material things. But this was not the message of the early church fathers. Nor was it the message of the men and women of faith who throughout history set church and nation aflame with revival.

The more we pursue such poppycock, the more likely we will end up like pampered children. Getting everything we want won't turn us into soldiers for Christ. We may wear a tailored suit with gold buttons and hash marks, but we will be no more soldiers than the six-year-old with his feet shoved in his dad's old combat boots and carrying a wooden gun. Unchecked, the prosperity-success syndrome will not see Christians developing together into a vigorous, stouthearted, indomitable church. Rather, it will reduce the body of Christ to spiritual flabbiness.[5]

Her message is important. Rather than the success doctrine being the ally of excellence, it is its enemy. To pursue earthly goals, no matter how enticing, is to be distracted from God's calling to excellence.

EXCELLENCE AND COMPARISON

Unless excellence is defined in a God-centered way, it will inevitably produce competition and comparison. When excellence is understood, as it usually is, to mean "superiority in a sphere of endeavor," the only points of reference are previous accomplishments and other people. The result is almost assuredly pride on the part of the successful and a sense of diminished self-worth for the less successful. Those who cannot compete become discouraged with themselves and resentful of God and others.

The effects of comparison are devastating. Satan compared himself to God, deceived himself, and ushered sin into the universe. Jacob compared Joseph to his brothers and set in motion an ugly train of fraternal hatred. The people of Israel compared themselves to the other nations, forsook God's unique purpose for them, and sought a king. Saul heard the people's comparison of David's feats with his own and his resultant bitterness poisoned his entire life. Whenever worth is based on comparison, the results are negative.

The same is true of competition. There is nothing inher"

ently wrong in competing with others. To test our skills and abilities against others is both stimulating and motivating. The danger comes when performance is considered to be the index of personal worth. If excellence is superiority, and excellence is my goal, then I must defeat my opponent or accept mediocrity. But such an attitude is intrinsically worldly. Kyle Rote, Jr. expresses a biblical view of competition when he says:

> I do not equate athletic success with personal worth. This is the great danger of competition for kids. They begin to think if they do not succeed in sports, they are failures as people. My opponent, whether the best player or the worst, still has the same eternal worth. We are special because God says we are special.[6]

The opposite danger to that mentioned by Rote also exists. People who do succeed in competition may believe that they are successes as people. But there is no correlation between the two. Excellence of achievement does not mean excellence of character.

A God-centered concept of excellence puts competition and comparison in their appropriate places. To be excellent means to realize God's purposes for one's life. Comparison is useful in that it stretches our vision and challenges us to realize our potential. Competition sharpens our skills. But another's achievements are not the benchmark for our lives. Neither is excellence or worth threatened or established by performances relative to another. Therefore, Peter's question to the Lord about John, "Lord, and what about this man?" received the direct rebuke, "What is that to you? You follow Me!" (John 21:21-22) Since excellence involves growth toward Christlikeness, the only adequate standard is the person of the Lord Jesus.

EXCELLENCE AND PERFECTIONISM

Closely allied to comparison is perfectionism. The perfectionist's standard of evaluation, however, is not the actual performances of others, but those of an idealized inner self. This individual is relentlessly driven to pursue exceptional standards, perhaps initially imposed by others but now thoroughly adopted as his own. Burns describes perfectionism as follows:

I do *not* mean the healthy pursuit of excellence by men and women who take genuine pleasure in striving to meet high standards. Without concern for quality, life would seem shallow and true accomplishments would be rare. The perfectionists I am talking about are those whose standards are high beyond reach or reason, people who strain compulsively and unremittingly toward impossible goals and who measure their own worth entirely in terms of productivity and accomplishment. For these people, the drive to excel can only be self-defeating.[7]

A perfectionist is someone whose pursuit of excellence has become obsessive since it is a means, not of pleasing God, but of providing a sense of self-worth.

Burns provides fascinating evidence that, on strictly pragmatic grounds, perfectionism is an enemy of excellence. He cites a study of insurance salesmen, which revealed that perfectionists who linked self-worth to achievement earned an average of $15,000 a year less than the nonperfectionist control group. A report on Olympic qualifiers among male gymnasts was similar. "The researchers found that the elite group tended to underemphasize the importance of past performance failures, while the athletes who failed to qualify were more likely to rouse themselves into near-panic states during competition through mental images of self-doubt and impending tragedy."[8] He also reports that perfectionism is allied with impaired productivity, emotional disturbances, impaired health, loneliness, and disturbed personal relationships. The root of the problem is imbedded in dichotomous, all-or-nothing thought patterns. The perfectionist is trapped in a "saint-or-sinner" syndrome, which sees partial success as total failure. Self-esteem is contingent on outstanding achievement and total competence.

The theological problem with perfectionism is that it denies the doctrine of progressive sanctification. The fallacy of the theological doctrine of perfectionism is self-evident. It cannot stand against the clear teaching of the Scriptures about sin in the believer's life (e.g., 1 John 1:5—2:2), and it denies twenty centuries of Christian experience. Moral perfection is the product of the Rapture and any claims of perfection in this life are the result of self-deception or rationalization. "Entire sanctification," "being perfected in love," "entire holiness," "fullness of faith"—all these theological attempts to claim perfection die the death of a thousand qualifications.

Psychological perfectionism, however, is far more subtle than theological perfectionism. Many staunch advocates of progressive sanctification are practicing perfectionists, committed to the belief that they are "supersaints." Compulsive achievers by nature, they sing of grace enthusiastically but are bound by legalism internally. Their dedication and commitment are equally impressive, but their perspective on life is not truly God-centered. As a result, the great truths of the New Covenant are known but not applied.

The alternative to perfectionism is the New Covenant principle, which was considered in chapter 9. It is important to draw attention to the fact that true excellence opposes, not applauds, perfectionism. The believer's excellence requires a heartfelt recognition that he is a clay pot containing a treasure. "Without Me, you can do nothing" is the believer's watchword. This means that unrealistic expectations of oneself and the compulsive-obsessive striving for self-imposed standards may lead away from, not toward, God's purpose. The "bionic believer" is not God's model of excellence.

EXCELLENCE AND POSITIVE THINKING

Many of the books on excellence fall into the positive mental attitude category. Excellence is a favorite word with motivators and inspirational possibility thinkers, who urge readers to "go for the gold." They counsel us to recognize that mediocrity is a terrible enemy, that the capacity for excellence lies within all of us, and that an individual who is willing to pay the price can achieve it. "Whatever the mind can conceive, a man can achieve," they urge. "As you pursue excellence, you will find that the world around you will have an almost uncanny way of stepping aside when you say, 'This is my goal. I am going to achieve it.' "[9]

There is a great deal that is valuable in the works of such men. They rightly stress the need for goals, the need to reach beyond the status quo, the importance of attitudes and priorities, and the value of an optimistic view of life. A positive, life-affirming perspective is an integral part of a biblical lifestyle, and the motivational school makes a valuable contribution in this way. Unfortunately, their work has a negative side, which has severe consequences. The problems in the approach of such men are so severe as virtually to debase their contributions.

The most serious problem is the thoroughly man-centered perspective. There is usually a religious appearance to this teaching, but the outlook is decidedly humanistic in orientation. One writer contends that "classic theology has erred in its insistence that theology be 'God-centered,' not 'man-centered.' "[10] The value systems that permeate the self-help books are rarely Christ-centered. For example, we are told that "total success is the continuing involvement in the pursuit of a worthy ideal, which is being realized for the benefit of others—rather than at their expense."[11] While this definition is more altruistic than most, it is entirely devoid of a divine or eternal perspective. Excellence demands that God's purpose and God's will be the focal point of all human endeavor. The living God is not merely a helpful addition to other principles of success. Rather, the fear of the Lord is the controlling principle of all skill in living (Prov. 9:10).

A related problem is the anemic and unbiblical view of faith found in motivational literature. Faith is a common term, but it is usually faith in the power of faith. "If you think you can, you can" may be an invigorating slogan, but is utterly meaningless. In such contexts, the word *faith* is emptied of biblical content. A Christian does not believe in the power of faith nor is he saved because of faith. He believes in the power of God and is saved by grace. Faith is only a channel; all virtue lies in God Himself. Yet such writers consistently quote or allude to biblical statements which entirely distort the meaning of Scripture. Waitley is typical. In a chapter entitled, "The Seed of Faith," he begins with a word of praise for faith and a reference to the Gospel:

> When we talk about faith—and belief—we have to refer to the greatest Book ever written, and the greatest Teacher of the ages on the subject. He summed it up when He said: "Go thy way; and as thou hast believed, so be it done unto thee."
>
> This simple statement cuts both ways, like a two-edged sword. Faith is the key to unlock the door of success for every human being. Or it is the lock that impris-

ons and keeps that human being from ever experiencing success. . . .

As a positive power, faith is the promise of the realization of things hoped for and unseen. As a negative power, it is the premonition of our deepest fears and unseen darkness.[12]

Waitley has totally distorted the Lord's words to the centurion in Matthew 8:13 (KJV). The Saviour was not giving a principle that "whatever one believes, one receives." He was granting the request of a Gentile man who had great faith in Him. Biblical faith is not a form of self-fulfilling prophecy or belief in oneself. It is unshakable confidence in the living God. Waitley's illustrations of faith are anecdotes of people who believed in themselves and in their goals. But the optimism with which Norman Cousins faced severe illness and the confidence with which Lee Trevino plays golf is not Christian faith. Positive self-talk and cheerful optimism is not what the Lord calls faith. Valuable as such qualities are, this transmutation of God-centered faith into man-centered, positive thinking is pernicious. Trust in an unworthy object is disastrous and cannot produce spiritual excellence.

A third major problem lies with the motivator's vision of success. Positive thinkers have a lot to say to achievers and the upwardly mobile, since they have adopted the American success value system. Their books are filled with rags-to-riches anecdotes. But there is little serious grappling with failure and suffering.

A fourth problem relates to priorities. Because positive thinkers lack a deep commitment to a biblical value system, they have little to say about how to determine priorities. Waitley quotes with approval some words of Thomas Wolfe:

> If we have a talent and cannot use it, we have failed. If we have a talent and use only half of it, we have partly failed. If we have a talent and learn somehow to use all of it, we have gloriously succeeded, and won a satisfaction and a triumph few individuals ever know.[13]

The initial part of Wolfe's statement is absurd. Every individual has talents he does not and never will use. In fact, an individual who attempted to use every talent to the fullest would be a total failure, if he did not first become the inmate of a mental institution. The real question is, "Which of my talents has priority?" The balancing of responsibilities requires divine wisdom and a harmonizing goal which embraces all of life. Only a God-centered life can know this.

The great fallacy, then, of the positive thinking school is its man-centeredness. Excellence demands a God-centered life and a God-centered view of life. When anyone or anything but the triune God is placed at the center of life, man cannot realize his divinely intended purpose.

CHAPTER TWELVE

GOING FOR THE GOLD

Every four years, for two weeks in the winter and again in the summer, the spotlight of world attention glares on the Olympic games. Millions around the world sit gripped by the spectacle of highly trained athletes competing at the limits of human ability, and new heroes such as Carl Lewis and Greg Louganis share the mantle of glory with such illustrious names as Jesse Owens, Emil Zatopek, Mark Spitz, and Olga Korbut. Others captivate the popular imagination because their athletic brilliance is coupled with an intense, almost superhuman determination.

In the 1976 Olympics in Montreal, a Japanese gymnast, Shun Fujimoto, was competing in the team competition. Somehow, during the floor exercises, he broke his right knee. It was obvious to all reasonable observers that he would be forced to withdraw. But they reckoned without the determination of a true competitor. On the following day, Fujimoto competed in his strongest event, the rings. His routine was excellent, but the critical point lay ahead—the dismount. Without hesitation, Fujimoto ended with a twisting, triple somersault. There was a moment of intense quiet as he landed with tremendous impact on his wounded knee. Then came thundering applause as he stood his ground. Later, reporters asked about that moment and he replied, "The pain shot through me like a knife. It brought tears to my eyes. But now I have a gold medal and the pain is gone."

GOING FOR THE GOLD

The world of sports is filled with such stories. I vividly remember listening to the finish of the marathon race in the 1954 British Empire games when an Englishman named Jim Peters entered the stadium miles ahead of the other competitors. But his pace had taken a terrible toll. It took fifteen painful minutes for him to travel the 300 yards from the entrance to the usual finish line. Twelve different times he collapsed to the track but eleven times he determinedly arose and staggered on. The final time he collapsed over the finish line into the arms of his trainer and lapsed into unconsciousness. Only much later did he realize that the marathon finish line was 200 yards farther away, on the other side of the track. He never finished the race, but the radio recount of the race and the newspaper photographs left etched on a young boy's mind an understanding of courage and commitment. So did a hockey player named Bobby Baun. Carried off the ice in a Stanley Cup playoff game with a serious leg injury, he returned after medical treatment to score the winning goal for the Toronto Maple Leafs. The following day, doctors discovered that the leg had, in fact, been broken. No one who watched tight end Kellen Winslow lead the San Diego Chargers to a heartstopping, double overtime, playoff victory over the Miami Dolphins will doubt that he played the greatest game ever by a football player, returning again and again from injury and exhaustion to make crucial catches.

Athletics provide an arena in which excellence is both recognizable and rewardable. Perhaps that is one reason why they are so popular. It is far harder to perceive what it means to be an excellent homemaker or parent. And the rewards are far less tangible, though no less real. There are no Olympic games or gold medals for Sunday School teachers or disciplemakers, at least in this life. And though some aspects of our vocation may be measurable by a standard of excellence, a biblical view of excellence begins with the hidden man of the heart, which only God sees but which He considers paramount, since "God sees not as man sees, for man looks at the outward appearance, but the Lord looks at the heart" (1 Sam. 16:7). These are dimensions of life which far transcend the excellence of an athlete.

Nevertheless, there is something about athletic competition that calls out the very best that an individual has to give.

A CALL TO EXCELLENCE

That is one reason why, in the New Testament, one of the most common and important illustrations of the Christian life is athletic competition. The Bible's illustrations are revealing since the way we see life determines the way we live life. Therefore, Christian living cannot be compared to a vacation or to a picnic. God has called us to spiritual warfare. Christian living takes place in the arena, in a competition demanding the very best we can give. And the reward is far more significant than a gold medal, a championship ring, or an inscription on the Stanley Cup. It is a perspective spelled out with great clarity in Paul's words in 1 Corinthians 9:24-27:

> Do you not know that those who run in a race all run, but only one receives the prize? Run in such a way that you may win. And everyone who competes in the games exercises self-control in all things. They then do it to receive a perishable wreath, but we an imperishable. Therefore I run in such a way, as not without aim; I box in such a way, as not beating the air; but I buffet my body and make it my slave, lest possibly, after I have preached to others, I myself should be disqualified.

In using an athletic metaphor, Paul was using an illustration familiar to the Corinthians. There were two great games in Greece: the Olympic and the Isthmian. The latter were held every two years, a short distance from Corinth, with the city as its patron. In fact, the games were held in A.D. 51, the very time Paul had evangelized Corinth, and perhaps that event inspired his illustration. The games were open only to Greeks of pure citizenship, and athletes competed in five major events—running, jumping, throwing (javelin and discus), boxing, and wrestling. Contestants were full-time athletes who devoted their lives to the goal of victory. For ten months, they trained on a daily basis, following a strict diet; in fact, athletes could be disqualified for failing to maintain strict adherence to the rules. The rewards were great. The immediate prize was a wreath made of twisted pine branches, but a winner also achieved heroic status. He was celebrated by the poets and honored by his city, for a community in which a champion resided was blessed by the gods. All of this is very familiar. Gold medal winners in our modern Olympics are inundated

154

with civic honors and opportunities for commercial endorse-ments. Millions of dollars and a future of prosperity, prestige, and security are the ways we award our modern heroes.

The facts of the Isthmian games were well known to the Corinthians, but Paul wants them to recognize a parallel to a far more significant sphere of life, the Christian race. It is an il-lustration which provides a rich summary of many elements of the biblical concept of excellence, and thus will serve as a help-ful review of the themes we have discovered in God's Word.

THE PURSUIT OF SPIRITUAL EXCELLENCE

Just as an athlete runs to win, so does the believer. We are called to "run with endurance the race that is set before us" (Heb. 12:1). But two important differences exist between an athletic race and the Christian race. First, athletics by their very nature involve competition with others—we win by de-feating another contestant. As Vince Lombardi is reputed to have said, "Winning isn't everything; it's the only thing." Football coach George Allen philosophized, "The pursuit of victory is my religion." The epitome of this attitude is a foot-ball game played between Georgia Tech and tiny Cumberland College in 1916. In the spring, Cumberland had upset the "Rambling Wrecks" in a homecoming baseball game. Humili-ated, Tech's football team determined to take revenge. The game was finally called in the third quarter with Cumberland unable to field enough uninjured players and trailing 222-0!

Such ruthless competitiveness is a tragic distortion. Competition can be healthy, causing us to give more than we thought possible; that's why records are far more likely to be set in the meet and not in practice. But the Christian life is not based on competition. We do not win by causing others to lose. The second and closely related difference is that athletic competition involves comparison with others. Such compari-son is natural and appropriate in sports, as long as it is not confused with personal worth. But similar comparisons in the spiritual realm are lethal, as is clearly illustrated in the sad case of King Saul. When he heard himself compared with David, and compared himself with David, he became consumed by jealousy and hostility, and a festering sore of bitterness poi-soned his spirit (1 Sam. 18:6-9).

"Run in such a way that you may win," exhorts Paul.

155

He is thinking neither of competition with others nor comparison to others, but rather of a commitment to spiritual excellence. Quite literally, Paul writes, "Run that you may lay hold," a phrase which echoes his use of the same word in his Epistle to the Philippians: "I press on in order that I may lay hold of that for which I was laid hold of by Christ Jesus" (Phil. 3:12). The Christian does not "win" by outdistancing others but by laying hold of God's pattern and purpose for his life. The Lord Jesus has called us to Christlikeness of character and to committed service for His glory. In other words, victory for the Christian is *spiritual excellence, the maximum exercise of our gifts and abilities within the range of responsibilities given by God.* This first applies to our character and then to our conduct.

Tom Landry has observed, "The quality of a life is in direct proportion to its commitment to excellence." If this is true of the Dallas Cowboys, it is far more true of the child of God. Running to win involves possessing a consuming desire to be the best we can be for the Lord Jesus Christ.

Michelangelo stands as one of the towering figures in the history of art. His majestic frescoes on the ceiling of the Sistine Chapel and his masterful sculptures bear witness to his greatness. But he was a man never content to rest on his laurels. He spent countless hours on his back on the scaffolding in the Sistine, carefully perfecting the details of each figure. When a friend questioned such meticulous attention to detail, on the grounds that "at that height, who will know whether it is perfect or not?" Michelangelo's simple response was, "I will." After completing what some consider his greatest work, *Moses,* the master sculptor stood back and surveyed his craftsmanship. Suddenly, in anger, he struck the knee of his creation with his chisel and shouted, "Why don't you speak?" The chisel scar that remains on the statue's knee is the mark of a man who always reached out for more. His ambition was to be the best he could be. The Christian adds a deeper dimension. His ambition is not simply to be good or to be good for something. He longs to be good for Someone, striving for excellence out of love for his Saviour.

THE PRACTICE OF SPIRITUAL EXCELLENCE

Excellence doesn't come cheaply. The Apostle Paul is not content to give us a general appeal: "Run to win." He specifies three factors indispensable in the training of a spiritual athlete. The first of these is *discipline:* "Everyone who competes in the games exercises self-control in all things" (1 Cor. 9:25). The word he uses to describe the competition is itself illuminating. *Agonizomai* is the Greek word from which we derive our word *agony* and indicates that Paul is thinking of an intense struggle, a grueling marathon. The Christian life is not a brief sprint, requiring short-range brilliance, but a distance race, demanding long-range determination and discipline. It is a battle against both external difficulties and internal attitudes, and only the disciplined and trained athlete will overcome. Therefore, the believer must exercise self-control in every area of life. This involves developing disciplined habits in the Word of God, in prayer, and in fellowship with other believers. The words of Hudson Taylor bear repetition: "A man can be spiritually consecrated and dedicated, and of very little use to God because his life is not disciplined." It must be noted, however, that the disciplined life is above all a Spirit-filled life. Rigorous self-discipline becomes little more than legalism apart from the enabling, empowering work of the Spirit.

A second requirement of a spiritual athlete committed to excellence is *direction:* "Therefore I do not run like a man running aimlessly" (1 Cor. 9:26, NIV). The runner in the Greek stadium focused on the square pillar which marked the end of the course. In the same way, Paul had no uncertainty about his fixed goal in life—to please and glorify God. It is obvious that a believer who loses sight of this goal will waste his efforts or waver in his commitments. A fanatic, we are told, redoubles his effort when he has lost his direction; similarly, someone has commented that man is the only animal who runs faster when he has lost his way. The central issue of life is not "What can I do?" but "Who do I want to be?" Discipline goes hand in hand with direction. Unless our lives are like arrows shot toward a target, they will have little impact; unless our discipline is consistent with our direction, we will have little value. An athlete sets aside legitimate pleasures because they may lead him away from his goal. So must a believer. As the philosopher John Locke warned, "He that knows not how to resist the importunity of present pleasure or pain for the sake of what reason tells him is fit to be done . . . is in danger of never being good for anything."

A CALL TO EXCELLENCE

It is important to remember that while excellence must always be our direction, it will never ultimately be our destination in this life. There will always be large areas of our lives which need tilling and weeding. Not long ago, a friend criticized an area of our church's ministry and complained that there seemed to be no commitment to excellence. His words stung, especially since I was working on this book at the time, but honest analysis left no doubt that he was right. We had a blind spot, and at best possessed a theoretical desire for excellence but little practical commitment to it. Very often, I have discovered that my desire for excellence in one area only makes my deficiencies in other areas more apparent. I am frustrated by my inadequacies and mediocrities. I seem to have so far to grow! If such a recognition of my shortcomings paralyzes me, I am defeated, and excellence becomes a hopeless idea. But if I commit myself in the direction of excellence, begin to cultivate it in my life while honestly acknowledging my weaknesses, and walk in confident dependence on the indwelling Spirit, His strength is perfected in my weakness (2 Cor. 12:9).

The third mark of a spiritual athlete, according to Paul, is *determination*. "I box in such a way, as not beating the air; but I buffet my body and make it my slave" (1 Cor. 9:26-27). Paul here shifts his illustration to that of boxing, which in the first century involved bare-fisted fighters, their hands wrapped with leather thongs, brawling to a finish, with only eye-gouging and biting prohibited. Their style was quite different from modern boxers. They whirled their arms in a windmill fashion, intent on hitting their opponent with their fists or at least lashing them with the thongs. Paul isn't interested in shadow-boxing or beating the air for show. His arms do not flail purposelessly. Nor is he careless. An untrained boxer will quickly fail and so Paul pummels his own body, beating it black and blue, not because it is his enemy but because it must be his servant. An athlete hardens his body, testing it to the limits, so that it will respond under stress. Christian living is no less demanding. Our bodies are not to be shackled in bonds, but kept in spiritual bounds, so that we can effectively serve the Saviour. There are times when everything within us will urge us to relax, to back off, to stop paying such a high price to serve Christ. At moments like that, when discouragement, fatigue, and difficulties flood in upon us, it is the believer who is disciplined and directed in his walk with the Lord Jesus who will have "the winner's edge."

But a caution must be sounded. True biblical excellence begins with what we are, not what we do. And true excellence requires balance. A one-sided intensity can often become the enemy, rather than the ally, of excellence. Christian excellence is essentially Christlikeness and this requires faithfulness in the whole range of responsibilities given by God.

It is always painful to point out the inadequacies of spiritual heroes, but sometimes it reveals in vivid form some danger signs in our own lives. C.T Studd was, by any standard of evaluation, a remarkable man. A brilliant athlete, a Cambridge scholar, and heir to a considerable fortune, he created a sensation in nineteenth-century England by dedicating his life and fortune to foreign missionary service. As one of the Cambridge Seven, he sailed to China in 1885 to serve his Lord. After ten difficult years, he returned, broken in health, to England. In 1900, he and his family sailed again, this time to India, where he served for six years before his health again suffered. But in 1912 he was off again, this time for Africa, to establish the Heart of Africa Mission in the Belgian Congo. He left his sick wife and four daughters in England, over her strong objections to his venture, and returned home only once, in 1916, before his death in 1931.

No one can doubt C.T. Studd's zeal for his Lord. He lived by his own words, "We do need to be intense, and our intensity must ever increase." That meant working eighteen-hour days, with no days off and no diverting activities. It was the Lord's work he was doing, and no sacrifice was too great to make for Him. The lethargy of most Christians toward the lost enraged him, and he determined to live with single-minded excellence for Jesus Christ.

But tragically, Studd's zeal consumed both him and those around him. It is impossible to justify his treatment of his wife, leaving her ill and living apart for eighteen years. His other relationships deteriorated as he made dictatorial demands on missionaries who came to serve under him. He even dismissed family members from the mission because he considered them less than totally committed, despite their sacrificial care of him in illness. The work was torn by doctrinal and personal controversies and fellow-workers were shocked by

Studd's attitude toward the African Christians. Tragically, his hard work and ill health caused him to turn to morphine for relief, and he finally became addicted to the drug. This was the final straw for the mission's home committee and they felt compelled to remove Studd from the mission which he founded.

It is sad to point to the downfall of a dedicated man who accomplished much good.[1] But it points to a fundamental issue. C.T. Studd was so intensely committed to a single aspect of God's truth that his intensity became destructive. He saw excellence in terms of what he did and that led him to miss God's will for the entire range of responsibilities God had given him. Christlikeness, true excellence, involves a balanced life and if a zeal for evangelism causes us to ignore our families or to become harsh and unloving with fellow-believers, excellence has been sacrificed to extremism. Studd's downfall has lessons for the business executive single-mindedly developing professional skill; for the pastor building a great church or preaching great sermons; for the scholar unrelentingly researching the book which will be his contribution to knowledge; to the mother pouring all her energy into her family and marriage. Worthy ambitions all, dedication to them can be destructive if it is not coupled with a prior commitment to godly character and a recognition of the full range of responsibilities to which God calls us.

THE PURPOSE OF SPIRITUAL EXCELLENCE

But why live such a life? According to Paul, there are two reasons, one positive and the other negative. First, there is *the privilege of reward:* "They then do it to receive a perishable wreath, but we an imperishable" (1 Cor. 9:25). The Greek athlete quite literally sought a fading wreath, but though a gold medal doesn't fade, it does tarnish. Past accomplishments quickly fade in meaning and significance. Yesterday's heroes are today's unknowns and the high euphoria of victory soon turns into the haunting question: "Is that all there is?" Olympic gold cannot fill the vacuum of empty hearts. But the believer seeks the imperishable crown of divine approval. There is coming a time when we believers will stand before the Lord Jesus and our present activities will be given eternal significance. How small many of our present concerns seem when weighed against eternity! If Olympic athletes pursue a fading wreath with discipline, direction, and determination, how much more should a believer live with such attributes before God!

A second incentive is *the possibility of disapproval:* "lest possibly, after I have preached to others, I myself would be disqualified" (1 Cor. 9:27). Paul is not fearful of losing his citizenship for violating the rule of competition. What Paul fears, as the word suggests, is disapproval, the loss of rewards, and exclusion from the prize. An athlete who is caught using steroids is stripped of his medals, no matter how impressive his achievements appear. A believer may apparently do much for the Lord but because he is not living in fellowship with the Lord Jesus, he will not hear the Saviour's words: "Well done, good and faithful servant." Therefore John exhorts us, "Now, little children, abide in Him, so that when He appears, we may have confidence and not shrink away from Him in shame at His coming" (1 John 2:28).

In some of the ancient Greek games, the winner was the man who crossed the finish line with his torch burning. It is one thing to finish, quite another to finish well. As the poet observes:

> Some men die in ashes,
> Some men die in flames,
> Some men die inch by inch,
> Playing little children's games.

How will we die? How are we living? We must go for the gold of God's approval!

This is the heart of all true excellence. Scripture is unrelentingly God-centered. Everything can and must be understood with reference to Him. He is the absolute standard by which all excellence is measured. Because He has purposed that all His regenerated people be conformed to the image of His Son, growth in Christlikeness is the essence of excellence in our present world. Such a life realizes God's purpose and gains God's approval.

This does not negate the importance of excellence of achievement. It is only to put first things first. When excellence of performance is the extension of an individual's charac-

ter, it has eternal value. Natural talents, spiritual gifts, person
al circumstances—all these reveal God's purpose for the individual Christian, and excellence involves developing and exercising such things as God's stewardship, in obedience to the
Lord's guidance and in dependence on His enabling. The excellent believer is therefore not necessarily the person who
establishes records, or who accomplishes great feats, or who
displays great skill. These are the facets of excellence, but not
the essence of it. It must be clearly understood: *The biblical
concept of excellence is conformity to God's purpose for the individual
believer, in character and in conduct.*

Such conformity cannot and will not be fully realized in
this life. Thus, excellence means an unending pursuit, a relent-
less quest, to actualize increasingly more of the divine purpose. Inspired by the love of God and a desire to glorify Him,
the Christian committed to excellence seeks to lay hold of more
and more of God's purpose. At the same time, the believer
realizes that God alone is excellent. The greatest excellence is
to be a clean vessel, fit for the Master's use. Because God's
purpose is to manifest His power through human weakness,
excellence does not consist of human perfection and adequacy.
It is not incompatible with human frailties and shortcomings.
To be excellent is to be authentic and transparent, since true
excellence lies in the treasure we contain, not the talents we
display. An obsessive, compulsive striving after self-fulfillment
or human acclaim cannot produce excellence. Only a passionate longing to glorify God and to realize His goals is consistent
with the biblical concept of excellence.

NOTES

Chapter One
1. R.B.Y. Scott, *Proverbs, Ecclesiastes*, Anchor Bible (Garden City, N.Y.: Doubleday, 1963), p. xvii.

Chapter Two
1. Plutarch, *Lives:* Alexander, 4:8.
2. *Oxford English Dictionary* 3:371
3. John Conway, "Standards of Excellence," in *Excellence and Leadership in a Democracy*, ed. Stephen R. Graubard and Gerald Holton (New York: Columbia University Press, 1962), p. 57. Italics mine.
4. Lance Morrow, "Have We Abandoned Excellence?" *Time*, March 22, 1982, p. 70.
5. Lawrence C. Becker, "The Neglect of Virtue," *Ethics* 85 (January 1975): 111.
6. Wallace C. Rusterholtz, "The Pursuit of Excellence," *Religious Humanism* 15 (Summer 1981): 107.
7. Attributed to Joseph L. Blau by David Norton, "Equality and Excellence in the Democratic Ideal" in *History, Religion, and Spiritual Democracy*, ed. Maurice Wohlgelernter (New York: Columbia University Press, 1980), p. 273.
8. Norton, p. 284.
9. Jerome Nathanson, *Individual Excellence and Social Responsibility* (Buffalo, N.Y.: Prometheus Books, 1974), p. 1.
10. Becker, pp. 112, 114.
11. John W. Gardner, *Excellence* (New York: Harper and Row, 1961), pp. 86, 144.
12. Ibid., pp. 193-195.
13. Ibid., p. 156.

14. Alasdair MacIntyre, *After Virtue: A Study of Moral Theology* (Notre Dame, Ind.: University of Notre Dame Press, 1981), p. 172.

15. Ibid., p. 163.

16. John Hospers, *Human Conduct: Problems of Ethics* (New York: Harcourt Brace Jovanovich, Inc., 1972), p. 86.

17. MacIntyre, p. 108.

18. Conway, pp. 65-66.

19. MacIntyre, p. 173.

20. Adam Yarmolinsky, "Explicit Recognition of Excellence," in Graubard and Holton, p. 146.

21. Thomas J. Peters and Robert H. Waterman, Jr., *In Search of Excellence* (New York: Harper and Row, 1982), p. 12.

22. Ibid., p. 13.

23. C.S. Lewis, *Mere Christianity* (London: Collins, 1952), p. 107.

24. Ibid., p. 108.

25. H. Richard Niebuhr, *Christ and Culture* (New York: Harper and Row, 1951), p. 6

Chapter Three

1. *Time*, March 22, 1982, p. 70.

2. Thomas J. Peters and Robert H. Waterman, Jr., *In Search of Excellence* (New York: Harper and Row, 1982), pp. xxi, 15, 280, 287, xxii.

3. Ibid., p. 285.

4. John W. Gardner, *Excellence* (New York: Harper and Row, 1961), p. 86.

5. Louis Berkhof, *Systematic Theology*, 4th rev. and enlarged edition (Grand Rapids: Wm. B. Eerdmans, 1941), p. 74.

6. Augustus H. Strong, *Systematic Theology* (Westwood, N.J.: Fleming H. Revell, 1907), p. 302.

7. A.W. Tozer, *The Knowledge of the Holy* (New York: Harper and Row, 1961), p. 113.

8. Bernard Ramm, *Them He Glorified* (Grand Rapids: Wm. B. Eerdmans, 1963), p. 89.

9. J.A. Schep, *The Nature of the Resurrection Body* (Grand Rapids: Wm. B. Eerdmans, 1964), p. 204.

10. Berkhof, p. 203.

11. Gary Inrig, *Life in His Body* (Wheaton, Ill.: Harold Shaw, 1975), p. 49.

12. Andrew A. Bonar, *Memoir and Remains of Robert Murray McCheyne* (Grand Rapids: Baker Book House, 1978), p. 123.

Chapter Four

1. Eli Ginzburg and John Herma, *Talent and Performance* (New York: Columbia University Press, 1973), p. 203.

2. John W. Gardner, *Excellence* (New York: Harper and Row, 1961), p. 109.

3. John Henry Jowett, source unknown.

4. Charles Bigg, *A Critical and Exegetical Commentary on the Epistles of St. Peter and Jude* (Edinburgh: T. & T. Clark, 1902), p. 134.

5. Gardner, pp. 178-179.

6. Philip Edgecombe Hughes, *Paul's Second Epistle to the Corinthians* (Grand Rapids: Wm. B. Eerdmans, 1962), p. 178.

7. S. Aaten, *New International Dictionary of New Testament Theology* (Grand Rapids: Zondervan, 1976), 2:47.

8. Cited in *The Life and Diary of David Brainerd*, ed. Jonathan Edwards (Chicago: Moody Press, 1980), pp. 244-245.

9. C.H. Spurgeon, *Autobiography: The Early Years* (Edinburgh: Banner of Truth, 1962), p. 208.

10. Gardner, pp. 101-102.

Chapter Five

1. Wes Neal, *The Handbook on Athletic Perfection* (Milford, Mich.: Mott Media, 1981), p. 72.

2. Charles Durham, *Temptation* (Downers Grove, Ill.: InterVarsity Press, 1982), pp. 159-160.

Chapter Six

1. Robert D. Foster, *The Navigator* (Colorado Springs: NavPress, 1983), p. 17.

2. Richard Nixon, *Leaders* (New York: Warner Books, 1982), p. 345.

3. Cited in W.H. Griffith Thomas, *Outline Studies in Matthew* (Grand Rapids: Wm. B. Eerdmans, 1961), p. 362.

Chapter Seven

1. Cited in William B. Lane, *Commentary on the Gospel of Mark* (Grand Rapids: Wm. B. Eerdmans, 1974), p. 339, n. 40.

2. Richard Nixon, *Leaders* (New York: Warner Books, 1982), p. 328.

3. Ibid., p. 330.

4. K. Hess, *New International Dictionaray of New Testament Theology* (Grand Rapids: Zondervan, 1978), 3:545.

5. H.W. Beyer, *Theological Dictionary of the New Testament* (Grand Rapids: Wm. B. Eerdmans, 1964), 2:82, 93.

6. Hess, p. 545.

7. Ibid., p. 544.

8. T.W. Manson, *The Church's Ministry* (London: Hodder and Stoughton, 1948), p. 27.

9. Thomas Torrance in *Theological Foundations for Ministry*, ed. Ray S. Anderson (Grand Rapids: Wm. B. Eerdmans, 1979), p. 715.

Chapter Eight

1. John W. Gardner, *Excellence* (New York: Harper and Row, 1961), pp. 109-110.

2. J.A. Motyer, *Philippian Studies: The Richness of Christ* (Chicago: InterVarsity Press, 1966), p. 127.

3. Thomas J. Peters and Robert H. Waterman, Jr., *In Search of Excellence* (New York: Harper and Row, 1982), p. 37.

4. Ibid., p. 13.

5. Harry A. Ironside, *Notes on Philippians* (New York: Loizeaux Brothers, 1946), p. 90.

6. James Fixx, *The Complete Book of Running* (New York: Random House, 1977), p. 92.

Chapter Nine

1. Murray Harris, "2 Corinthians" in *The Exposition Bible Commentary* (Grand Rapids: Zondervan, 1976), 10:342.

2. James Denney, *The Second Epistle to the Corinthians* (New York: A.C. Armstrong and Son, 1894), p. 159.

3. Philip Edgecombe Hughes, *Paul's Second Epistle to the Corinthians* (Grand Rapids: Wm. B. Eerdmans, 1962), p. 137.

4. Denney, p. 160.

5. Helmut Thielicke, *Between Heaven and Earth* (New York: Harper and Row, 1965), pp. 185-186.

6. Hughes, pp. 138-139.

7. F.F. Bruce, *1 and 2 Corinthians* (London: Oliphants, 1971), p. 197.

8. R.V.G. Tasker, *The Second Epistle of Paul to the Corinthians* (Grand Rapids: Wm. B. Eerdmans, 1958), pp. 73-74.

9. Denney, pp. 168-169.

10. Margery Williams, *The Velveteen Rabbit* (New York: Doubleday, 1958), pp. 16-17.

Chapter Ten

1. Thomas J. Peters and Robert H. Waterman, Jr., *In Search of Excellence* (New York: Harper and Row, 1982), p. 77.

2. Ibid., p. 323.

3. Ibid., p. xxii.

4. Ibid., pp. 84-85.

5. John W. Gardner, *Excellence* (New York: Harper and Row, 1961), pp. 114-115.

6. Ibid., p. 120.

7. Douglas Hyde, *Dedication and Leadership* (Notre Dame, Ind.: University of Notre Dame Press, 1966), p. 27.

8. Ibid., pp. 20-21.

9. Os Guiness, *The Gravedigger File* (Downers Grove, Ill.: InterVarsity Press, 1983), p. 36.

10. George Eldon Ladd, *A Theology of the New Testament* (Grand Rapids: Wm. B. Eerdmans, 1974), pp. 107-108.

11. Robert Coleman, *The Master Plan of Evangelism* (Old Tappan, N.J.: Fleming H. Revell, 1964), p. 50.

12. Lawrence Richards and Gib Martin, *A Theology of Personal Ministry* (Grand Rapids: Zondervan, 1981), p. 222.

13. Peters and Waterman, p. 26.

14. John W. Gardner, *No Easy Victories* (New York: Harper and Row, 1968), p. 41.

15. Ibid., p. 44.

16. James MacGregor Burns, *Leadership* (New York: Harper and Row, 1978), p. 1.

17. Gardner, *Victories*, p. 42.

18. Peter Drucker, *The Effective Executive* (New York: Harper and Row, 1967), p. 57.

19. Burns, p. 455.

20. Leon Morris, *The First Epistle of Paul to the Corinthians* (Grand Rapids: Wm. B. Eerdmans, 1958), p. 174.

21. Robert Thomas, *Understanding Spiritual Gifts* (Chicago: Moody Press, 1978), p. 61.

22. Cited in Michael Green, *Evangelism in the Early Church*

(Grand Rapids: Wm. B. Eerdmans, 1970), p. 179
23. Ibid., p. 180.

Chapter Eleven
1. Vernon C. Grounds, "What's So Great About Success?" *Leadership*, 2 (Winter 1981): 54.
2. Ibid., p. 55.
3. Os Guiness, *The Gravedigger File* (Downers Grove, Ill.: InterVarsity Press, 1983), p. 129.
4. Joe Magliato, *The Wall Street Gospel* (Eugene, Ore.: Harvest House, 1981), pp. 142, 144.
5. Florence Bulle, *God Wants You Rich and Other Enticing Doctrines* (Minneapolis: Bethany House, 1983), p. 41.
6. Cited in Gary Warner, *Competition* (Elgin, Ill.: David C. Cook, 1979), p. 319.
7. David D. Burns, "The Perfectionist's Script for Self-Defeat," *Psychology Today*, November 1980, p. 34.
8. Ibid., p. 37.
9. Ted W. Engstrom, *The Pursuit of Excellence* (Grand Rapids: Zondervan, 1982), p. 29.
10. Robert Schuller, *Self-Esteem—The New Reformation* (Waco, Texas: Word Books, 1982), p. 64.
11. Denis Waitley, *Seeds of Greatness* (Old Tappan, N.J.: Fleming H. Revell, 1983), p. 148.
12. Ibid.
13. Ibid., p. 96.

Chapter Twelve
1. For a brief summary of Studd's life, see Ruth A. Tucker, *From Jerusalem to Irian Jaya* (Grand Rapids: Zondervan, 1983), pp. 263-268.